Global Mergers
and Acquisitions

Global Mergers and Acquisitions

Combining Companies Across Borders

Abdol S. Soofi and Yuqin Zhang

businessexpert
Press

First published in 2014 by
Business Expert Press, LLC
222 East 46th Street, New York, NY 10017
www.businessexpertpress.com

ISBN-13: 978-1-60649-774-6 (paperback)
ISBN-13: 978-1-60649-775-3 (e-book)

Business Expert Press Finance and Financial Management Collection

Collection ISSN: 2331-0049 (print)
Collection ISSN: 2331-0057 (electronic)

Cover and interior design by Exeter Premedia Services Private Ltd., Chennai, India

First edition: 2014

10 9 8 7 6 5 4 3 2 1

Printed in the United States of America.

Abdol Soofi dedicates this book to his wife Xing, to his daughter Rima, to his son Shauheen, and to the loving memory of his son Rosteen.

Yuqin Zhang dedicates this book to her father Wenhai Zhang, her husband Hongbin Dong, and her daughter Yicheng Dong

Abstract

This book primarily deals with corporate restructuring through mergers and acquisitions (M&As). It critically examines all functions that must be performed in completing an M&A transaction. Domestic and cross-border M&A's are very similar in many respects even though differences between them also exist. To include discussions of the issues that arise in cross-border M&A transactions, the book also covers discusses such as international finance and multinational financial management.

Given the increasing importance of China as the second largest economy in the world and Chinese companies' growing merger and acquisition (M&A) activities globally, we devote the last two chapters of the book to China's outward foreign direct investment and cross-border M&A activities. The case studies regarding Chinese foreign direct investment both in Greenfield and acquisition forms give additional insights into challenging tasks of due diligence and post-merger cultural integration that foreign investors face.

The knowledge of these topics is absolutely imperative in M&A decision making. Tasks include developing a strategy for merger or acquisition, finding a target, conducting due diligence, valuing the target company, conducting negotiations and structuring the deal, and, finally, satisfactorily meeting the most challenging phase of an M&A transaction; that is, integrating the acquiring and acquired companies. In short, the book is written as a concise guideline for those readers who are interested in gaining a clear understanding of what a merger or acquisition entails.

The M&A literature is a fragmented field of inquiry. The book brings together important, practical insights from this vast literature in a short, but cohesive form that hopefully has great managerial relevance.

Keywords

business valuation, cost of capital, cross-border acquisition, cultural integration deal structuring, exchange rate, FDI and national security, foreign direct investment, merger and acquisition, strategy, target selection, real options, regulatory agencies

Contents

Preface

This book primarily deals with corporate restructuring through mergers and acquisitions (M&As). It critically examines all functions that must be performed in completing an M&A transaction. Domestic and cross-border M&A's are very similar in many respects even though differences between them also exist. To include discussions of the issues that arise in cross-border M&A transactions, the book also discusses topics such as international finance and multinational financial management.

Given the increasing importance of China as the second largest economy in the world and Chinese companies' growing merger and acquisition (M&A) activities globally, we devote the last two chapters of the book to China's outward foreign direct investment and cross-border M&A activities. The case studies regarding Chinese foreign direct investments, both in Greenfield and acquisition forms, give additional insights into challenging tasks of due diligence and post-merger cultural integration that foreign investors face.

Throughout these discussions, we will emphasize methods, analytical tools, and concepts that have great applicability in M&As. This means that we would deliberately avoid broad theoretical discussions that do not have immediate relevancy for practical applications, even though knowing them might provide great theoretical insights into all sundry aspects of merging or acquiring another company or being acquired by another enterprise. It should not be construed from this emphasis on practical applications that theory is insignificant. On the contrary, we greatly value theory. This approach is based on our belief that business education should emphasize practical relevancy for the conduct of business and managerial decision making.

Based on this philosophy, we selected those topics because the knowledge of them absolutely imperative in M&A decision making. Naturally, a corporate executive cannot implement all tasks that are required to develop a strategy for merger or acquisition, to find a target, to conduct due diligence, to value the target company, to conduct negotiations and structure the deal, and, finally, satisfactorily meet the most challenging phase of an M&A transaction; that is, to integrate the acquiring and acquired companies. Accomplishing those tasks requires a great deal of resources and expertise: consulting companies, law firms that specialize in M&As, and investment banks should be consulted to accomplish the tasks. However, the decision maker should have an understanding and a clear overview of all aspects of the processes that a typical merger or acquisition initiative must go through. This book is written as a concise guideline for those readers who are interested in gaining a clear understanding of what a merger or acquisition entails.

Reviewing the M&A literature, one comes across a fragmented field of inquiry. One can clearly recognize different patterns in the development of the M&A literature according to the disciplines of the researchers. The research interests in M&A and corporate restructuring literature are primarily concerned with the following questions. Why do companies merge? Are M&As successful in achieving the goals of acquisition and combinations? Why do so many companies fail to create shareholder value or capture the synergies they inspired to gain? How to best value the target firm? What role does postmerger integration play in postmerger performance of the acquiring and acquired companies? What role corporate and societal cultures play in the success or failure of M&As? These are among many other questions the literature on M&A deals with.

The fragmentary nature of the literature emerges from the discipline-based approach researchers take in answering the questions. One finds articles with emphasis on economics of M&A (economies of scale, market power, and shortcut to obtaining costly technology) written by economists; articles written by strategic management scholars focusing on motives for acquisition and postmerger performance according to the motives of consolidations; articles written by scholars in corporate finance, concentrating on postmerger performance based on stock market indicators. Studies by researchers on organization theory project attention on postmerger integration and conflicts arising during the integration processes and, finally, experts on human resources have focused on effective communications, cultural differences, and sociopsychological issues that might have an impact on the success or failure of the combined entities. Based on this, it is common knowledge among the scholars of M&As

that the discipline-based approach used for answering any of these questions leads to answers that tend to differ and in some cases even contradict each other (Larsson and Finkelstein 1999).

In this book, we review the literature of M&A from different angles and bring together important, practical insights from this vast literature in a short, but cohesive form that hopefully has great managerial relevance.

Structure of the Book

Cross-border M&As are international activities. To gain a better understanding of the depth and breadth of international business and economic transactions, Chapter 1 deals with globalization or internationalization of economies. In Chapter 2, we define some M&A terminologies, briefly review the motives for M&As, discuss different types of mergers, and differentiate between domestic and cross-border M&As. Chapter 3 gives an overview of M&A processes and reviews problems that often arise during acquisition processes. In Chapter 4, we develop strategies for M&As, define organizational culture, enumerate a set of strategic objectives for M&As, identify the corporate development office as the responsible body in many M&As by several companies, and elaborate on the role of the lead adviser in implementing mergers or acquisitions. Chapter 5 encompasses selecting a potential target for acquisition, enumerate target screening criteria, and defines as well as lists different types of due diligence.

Chapter 6 discusses accounting for M&As and, by means of examples, illustrates how valuation of the target firm will affect the income statement and balance sheet of the combined company. Chapter 7 deals with alternative approaches to valuation of the target firm by illustrative examples of comparable companies approach, the discount cash flow approach, the capital budgeting method, and free cash flow calculations under different assumptions about the growth of cash flows. Chapter 8 examines the important role the cost of capital plays in valuation methods. Chapter 9 considers real option analysis as a versatile method for valuing target companies in general; Chapter 10 closely examines how the Black–Scholes model is used in valuing target companies under different scenarios.

In Chapter 11, we turn our attention to valuing target companies in cross-border M&As, by discussing issues related to international finance. We examine the purchasing power parity theorem and real exchange rate, exchange rate fluctuations, and forward as well as swap currency transactions in the chapter. Moreover, we discuss the effect of currency fluctuations on the discounted cash flows of multinational companies in Chapter 11 too.

Chapter 12 handles the negotiation and deal structuring part of the acquisition process. It focuses on developing a strategy to secure approval from the target firm, refining valuation of the target, and developing a plan for financing the deal. Chapter 13 examines the important topic of postmerger integration and reorganization. Furthermore, the chapter focuses on different types of integration, approaches to integration, establishing a new organization, integration of functional departments of corporations; and instructs how to form a new corporate culture.

Part II of the book involves discussions of outbound M&A activities of China's enterprises, which until the last few years only involved state-owned enterprises. In Chapter 14, after a discussion of outward FDI by Chinese companies, we review factors that have contributed to outward M&A investment by China. Furthermore, the chapter examines the role of the Chinese government in promotion and regulation of outbound M&A activities of Chinese enterprises. Moreover, the chapter reviews the accounting method of business combinations in China. Finally, Chapter 15 examines major issues in Chinese cross-border M&A activities, including postmerger experiences of Chinese firms, rules for overseas acquisitions by Chinese firms, perceptions of Chinese executives in acquiring firms in developed countries, policies of host countries toward Chinese firms acquiring businesses in their countries, and experiences of Chinese firms in outward investment and acquisitions.

We thank Mr. Scott Isenberg, the Executive Acquisitions Editor, Business Expert Press for his leadership in development of this project and for encouraging us to write the book.

PART I

Cross-Border Mergers, Acquisitions, and Corporate Restructuring

CHAPTER 1

Internationalization
of Economies

It is commonly believed that among all factors affecting businesses, internationalization, or globalization of the economies, had the most profound impact on private business management since the Second World War. Of course, the subject of this book, cross-border mergers and acquisitions (M&As), is an important component of the internationalization or integration of diverse economic systems. Accordingly it is pivotally important to have a clear understanding of internationalization of the economies. We elaborate this important concept in this introductory chapter by examining the constituent parts of the internationalization process.

Internationalization of Product and Service Markets

It is common to use sum of exports X and imports M as a percentage of the gross domestic product (GDP) of a country as a measure of openness of the economy. According to this indicator, a rapid rise in international trade has occurred around the globe since World War II. We present values of the exports plus imports of goods and services as percentages of GDPs by types of economies since 1980 in Table 1.1.

As can be seen from Table 1.1, the degree of openness for all economies not only has increased drastically but with the exception of openness for the transition economies has been consistently on the rise over the last three decades. Of course, the rise in the openness index in an environment where both GDP and international trade were on the rise can only mean that the value of international trade is increasing at a faster rate than the rate of increase in the value of the GDP.

Table 1.1 Openness of the economies, $\dfrac{(X + M)}{GDP}$: 1980–2012

Year	World	Developing economies	Transition economies	Developed economies
1980	39.704	50.143	12.82	39.749
1990	38.369	50.202	26.782	36.334
2000	49.133	67.114	78.494	43.59
2010	59.07	72.532	63.047	53.448
2012	62.626	71.833	65.237	57.002

Source: UNCTAD Stat (2013).

It should be noted that internationalization in services implies internationalization of transportation, tourism, telecommunications, banking, insurance, and other professional services.

The world trade data in all commercial services indicate that between 2000 and 2011, the value of all commercial service exports increased from $1491 billion to $4349.9 billion, an increase of 191.75 percent. Furthermore, the value of imported commercial services world-wide increased from $1463.8 billion to $4152.3 billion, an increase of 183.66 percent during the same period (World Trade Organization 2013).[1]

Internationalization of Financial Markets

An important contributing factor to rapid internationalization process over the last three decades is the removal of restrictions on capital flows across the national borders of many countries. With the removal of the restrictions on capital flows, the sum of value of equity markets' capitalization, corporate and public bonds, and loans globally has increased from 12 trillion dollars in 1980 to 225 trillion in March 2013 (Lund et al. 2013).

International Transfers of Technology

International transfer of technology has increased through cross-border licensing agreements, cross-border M&As, joint ventures, foreign direct investment in wholly foreign-owned enterprises, and joint research and development (R&D) activities of multinational enterprises.

Internationalization of National Enterprises

An important aspect of internationalization of national enterprises, which began in the late nineteenth century and accelerated in the twentieth century, is global operations of what Alfred Chandler, Jr. (1984) called integrated industrial enterprises. The first step in the development of integrated international enterprises was the formation of an *administrative organization*. The pattern of development of these industrial enterprises and creation of the administrative organization is best described by Chandler:

> It was essential first to recruit a team to supervise the process of production, then to build a national and very often international sales network, and finally to set up a corporate office of middle and top managers to integrate and coordinate the two. Only then did the enterprise become multinational. Investment in production abroad followed, almost never preceded, the building of an overseas marketing network. (Chandler Jr. 1984, 491–492)

Multinational enterprises can fall into one of two categories: multidomestic and global. The *multidomestic enterprises* operate on stand-alone, country-centered management strategy. The enterprise is present in many countries but competes on a country-by-country basis. These enterprises operate in retailing, retail banking, insurance, and consumer packaged goods industries.

Global enterprises, on the other hand, adopt the strategy of integrating operations on a worldwide basis. The enterprise's competitive position in one country significantly affects and is affected by its position in other countries. The global enterprises operate in industries such as automobile, consumer electronics, semiconductors, and similar type of industries.

In addition to the rise of multinational enterprises, an increasing number of international coalitions and alliances among business entities for undertaking R&D, marketing, logistics, operations, and services have been formed in recent decades. These coalitions and alliances consist of joint ventures, licensing agreements, supply contracts, marketing agreements, and pooling of R&D activities.

Internationalization of the Labor Market

Internationalization of the labor market implies that the actors in the labor markets, that is, both the employers and suppliers of labor (workers), instead of entering the national labor markets interact in the global labor markets. Internationalization of the labor market also refers to the consequences of cross-border movements of goods, services, and capital as well as consequences of internationalization of production for the labor market. In short, internationalization of labor has taken place because of increased movement of work and labor across national boundaries. Specifically internationalization of labor over the last several decades has increased through rise in international trade, foreign investment, technology transfer, and increased mobility of people borders.

Clearly, not all immigrants enter the labor force of the host nation. This implies that only a portion of overall immigrants will enter in labor markets of the host countries. The data for the number of working immigrants globally is not available. Hence, we cite the stock of world immigrants as an indicator of the size of immigrants participating in the labor forces around the globe. Based on this we see that, for example, the stock of world migrants in mid-1990 is estimated to be 155,518,065. The number has increased to 213,943,812 in 2010, according to the United Nations (2013). This implies an average annual growth rate of 1.8 percent in stock of world total migration a portion of which constitutes labor force migration.

Internationalization of Communication and Transportation

Advances in communication and transportation technologies, mostly brought about by innovations in information technology (IT), have facilitated transnational movements of goods, services, and capital. These technological advances had and continue to have profound impacts on business organization, structure of industry, internationalization, and cross-border trade of services as well as cross-border M&As.

Having a clear definition for information technology, a term that is used frequently in the book will prove to be useful. Information technology refers "…to the interconnected set of technological and organizational innovations in electric computers, software engineering, control systems, integrated circuits, and telecommunications, that have made it possible to collect, generate, analyze, and diffuse large quantities of information at a minimal cost" (Miozzo and Soete 2001, 160).

It should be noted that internationalization of the economies to a large extent is made possible through services in general and via advances in IT and telecommunication services in particular, services that have been supplied with rapidly falling costs of production. Therefore, we find further discussions of the role services play in internationalization processes important, and we turn to discussions of these developments next.

What is the definition of services? A useful definition of the term refers to services as goods that are consumed at the time and location of the transaction. However, services are heterogeneous and the definition given here is not specific with respect to nature and categories of services. To have a clear understanding of which human activities constitute services and to gain insights into the important role these activities have played and are playing in internationalization of the economies, we discuss categories of services.

Even though there is no consensus on how to classify services, a technology-based taxonomy of services might be useful (Miozzo and Soete 2001). The technology-based taxonomy of services views services based on their intra- and inter-industry linkages. According to this taxonomy, services consist of the following types. First, personal services (restaurants, laundry, and beauty), and public and social services (health, education, and public administration); second, scale-intensive physical networks (transport, travel, and wholesale trade and distribution) and information network sectors (finance, insurance, and communications); and third, science-based and specialized supplier sectors (electronics and pharmaceutical).[2]

What is the mechanism by which advances in IT, specifically telecommunication services, affect internationalization of the economies? To answer this question, we need to define two characteristics of services: nonstorability and intangibility.

Nonstorability implies that services must be produced and consumed at the location and at the point of time the exchange is to take place. Intangibility refers to the uncertainty about the quality of services, which requires an ongoing interaction between the trading partners (Miozzo and Soete 2001).

Information technology increases transportability of services by eliminating or reducing the constraints of space and time of production and consumption, that is, by producing services at one place and consuming them simultaneously at another location. As an example, we may cite delivery of a lecture via the Internet, where the instructor and students are located at separate locations. Another example is an IT specialist who remotely connects to the network of a client in a perhaps far away location to perform a service.

Along with reduction in the nonstorability characteristic of services, the growing complexity of production and distribution of goods in the manufacturing sector has increased the service content of products. These services include R&D, design, marketing, distribution, and after-sales services that are essential inputs for many globally competitive enterprises.

With the steadily decreasing costs of communication, computing, and IT; increasing relaxation of controls on cross-border capital flows; and deregulation of industries in many countries, cross-border transactions of services have increased drastically in recent decades.

As a result of these technological developments, an important international market for M&A has also emerged. In this expanding global market, firms aim to take full advantage of their competitive advantages. Mergers and acquisitions, mostly acquisitions, appear to be the most efficient, and some believe a less expensive vehicle for the global presence of many enterprises.

Understanding the internationalization of the economies as discussed above is an important task in the development of strategies for acquiring another enterprise in domestic or international markets.

Summary

This chapter dealt with the rapid pace of internationalization of economies over the last several decades. The discussions involve internationalization of products, services, financial markets, technology transfers, labor markets, communications, and transportation. It was pointed out that as a result of the changes in information and communication technologies, cross-border M&A is becoming an increasingly popular strategy for growth and profitability by many enterprises.

CHAPTER 2

Mergers, Acquisitions and Corporate Restructuring

Research has shown that mergers and acquisitions (M&As) are effective means of entry into high-growth markets, generating cash in the short run, gaining advantages over the competitors without expanding production capacity. Furthermore, it is argued that M&As are efficient methods of acquisition of expertise, new technology, products, brands, and skilled employees. It is also believed that M&As reduce risks and assist internal product and process innovation (Brock 2005).

To set the foundation for the subsequent discussions of M&A, in this chapter, we will define terminologies of mergers, acquisitions, and corporate restructuring, discuss motives for M&As, identify risks associated with cross-border M&As, discuss different types of mergers, and differentiate domestic and cross-border M&As.

Types of Mergers and Acquisitions, and Terminologies Used in Business Combinations

We start with a definition of corporate restructuring and examine the various forms in which it appears.

Corporate restructuring activities may be classified into two categories: operational and financial. Operational restructuring involves changes in the firm's asset structure, which may take place by acquiring another business, by complete or partial sale of a business, by spin-off of a subsidiary or product line, or by downsizing unprofitable operations and units. Financial restructuring refers to those activities of the firm, which change its debt and equity structure. These activities include leveraged buyouts, management buyouts, reorganization, liquidation, and stock buyback. We focus on operational restructuring in this book.

Operational restructuring activities assume many forms. They could be workforce reduction or realignment, joint venture, or strategic alliance; divestitures; spin-off; carve-out; and takeover or buyout. The takeover or buyout could be friendly or hostile. The friendly takeover could be merger, consolidation, or acquisition of assets. The hostile takeover is completed by a hostile tender offer. Finally, merger could be in statutory form or in subsidiary form.

A *statutory merger* takes place when the acquiring or surviving company automatically becomes the owner of the assets and liabilities of the target firm according to the laws of the land or laws of the state in the United States, where the combined company is incorporated. A *subsidiary merger* occurs when a subsidiary of the acquiring firm becomes the owner of the assets and liabilities of the target. The acquiring firm is called a parent. The advantage of a subsidiary merger is avoidance of subjecting the acquiring company to the liabilities of the target.

The Terminologies of Corporate Restructuring

We define terminologies of corporate restructuring and foreign direct investment (FDI) in this section.

1. **Merger:** Any transaction that forms one business enterprise by two or more formerly independent business entities is called a merger. This implies that one company legally absorbs all assets and liabilities of another company. Mergers have the following characteristics. First, they are negotiated deals that meet certain technical, legal requirements; second, they are often friendly but one firm may be stronger and dominate the transaction.[1]
2. **Consolidation:** Corporate consolidation is a special form of merger. Corporate consolidation combines two business entities and creates a new enterprise. For example, companies A and B consolidate and form a new C Company.
3. **Acquisitions:** An acquisition refers to the purchase of a controlling interest in a firm, and involves a transfer of ownership.
4. **Tender Offers:** In a tender offer, one firm or person makes an offer directly to the shareholders of the target to buy their shares at

specified prices. A tender offer is hostile when an offer is made to the shareholders without approval of the board of directors of the target firm.

5. **Restructuring:** Corporate restructuring refers to changes in organization, operations, policies, and strategies to enable the firm to achieve its long-term objectives.

6. **Spin-off:** In spin-off transactions, some parent company's shareholders receive shares in a subsidiary in return for relinquishing their parent company shares.

7. **Split-up:** A split-up is the division of a company into two or more separate companies. It is different than spin-off because it involves the entire company rather than a subsidiary.

8. **Equity Carve-out:** An equity carve-out is a transaction in which a parent firm offers some of a subsidiary's common stock to the general public to bring in cash infusion to the parent without the parent's loss of control.

9. **Divestitures:** Divestitures involve the sale of a segment of a company (assets, product line, and a subsidiary) to another party for cash and or securities.

10. **Industry Roll-ups:** In an industry roll-up, the consolidator acquires a large number of small companies with similar operations. Profit maximization or revenue maximization is achieved by economies of scale in purchasing, marketing, information systems, distribution, and senior management.

11. **Takeovers or buyouts:** Takeovers or buyouts refer to a change in controlling ownership of a corporation.

12. **Leveraged Buyouts:** In a leveraged buyout, a small group of investors purchases a target company by financing the acquisition largely by borrowed funds.

13. **Leveraged Recapitalization:** Leveraged recapitalization is a defensive reorganization of the company's capital structure (the combination of a company's short-term and long-term debts, as well as common and preferred stocks) in which outside shareholders (non-management shareholders) receive a large, one-time cash dividend and inside shareholders (shares held by the managers of the firm) receive new shares of stock instead.

14. **Greenfield Investment:** Greenfield investment project refers to investment in a new project in a host country involving the construction of a new building (or leasing of an existing building), purchasing of new machinery and equipment, hiring of managers, administrative staff, and production workers. In short, in a greenfield investment the investors create a new business entity.
15. **Cross-border M&A:** Cross-border M&As are FDI through which an existing business in part or in its entirety is acquired in a host country.
16. **Foreign direct investment (FDI):** DFI refers to investment in a foreign country and can assume greenfield or cross-border M&A form.

Reasons for Corporate Restructuring

The fundamental reason for corporate restructuring is achieving the goals of the business entity that initiates the restructuring policy. Most analysts consider profit maximization (using the terminology of financial literature, wealth maximization) as the goal of private enterprises. In achieving the goal, enterprises adopt different objectives in capturing operating synergy and financial synergy.

In M&As, operating synergies are created by economies of scale and economies of scope. Economies of scale refer to lowering of the long-run average cost of production as the firm's output expands. Economies of scope occur when a firm produces products that use similar types of inputs. As an example, we may think of a firm using sheets of steel in the production of refrigerators as well as washers and dryers. Both products use the same kind of input, in this example the steel sheets. The economies of scope are created if a company that only produced refrigerators also begins production of washers and dryers.

Financial synergy, on the other hand, occurs when the acquisition of a target firm lowers the cost of capital of the acquiring firm. Financial synergy may be classified into a number of categories including synergy resulting from diversification, strategic realignment, managerial hubris, purchasing undervalued assets, mismanagement, managerialism, tax considerations, and market power. We discuss each of these categories that create financial synergy next.

Diversification happens when an acquirer buys a target firm outside of its current primary lines of business. Diversification could occur in a number of ways such as buying a target firm, which expands markets for an existing product or if such acquisition creates a new product for the current market, or if the acquisition leads to the creation of new products for new markets.

Synergy from strategic realignment takes place when firms use M&As to rapidly adjust to the changing economic environments. Most of the forces that cause such rapid external changes are changing government regulations and technological changes.

Hubris creates synergy, albeit a negative one for the acquiring entity, because of overoptimistic valuation of the target by the management of the acquiring company. Due to the overestimated value of the target, especially in a competitive bidding environment, and over self-confidence, the winner of the bid ends up in a value destroying acquisition.

Synergy created by buying undervalued assets is due to the purchase of a target firm when the cost of acquisition of the target is less than the cost of purchasing the assets the acquiring firm intends to replace. This condition occurs when the stock value of an enterprise falls substantially below its assets' book value (historical cost).

Mismanagement or agency problem refers to a situation where the management of an enterprise takes certain actions that are in their own best interest rather than the interest of the stockholders. Clearly, the agency problem arises from the separation of management and owners of an enterprise.

It is instructive to discuss the emergence of what Alfred Chandler called managerial capitalism. Chandler (1984) argues that as late as the mid-1800s, managers of major business enterprises were in fact the owners of the enterprises they managed. It was only in the 1850s and 1860s that the administrative hierarchies in large corporations grew to coordinate mass production and distribution of goods that were made possible by the newly constructed railroad and communication (telegram) systems. To manage such large integrated industrial enterprises, managerial capitalism became necessary for the first time in the United States.

Managerialism is a theory, which argues that managers acquire other business entities to increase their prestige, raise their income, to increase their sphere of influence, or for self-preservation.

Tax considerations, as a theory for M&As indicates that the acquiring firms could use accumulated losses from investment in M&A to reduce the income tax liabilities emanating from the future profits derived from the acquisition.

Market power hypothesis asserts that firms engage in M&A activities to reduce competition and increase their market power so that they could set higher prices by reducing the output.

In addition to these generalized hypotheses concerning motivation for M&As, we will discuss specific motives for cross-border M&A activities of Chinese firms in Chapter 14, Part II of the book.

Risks Associated with Cross-Border M&As

Cross-border M&As are international business activities and as such involve a number of risks that are associated with FDI. We enumerate and discuss the risks associated with FDI next.

1. Management risk:
   Smooth functioning of a newly acquired firm abroad requires placing a new management team at the helm. Often the formation of a new management team for an acquired enterprise requires combining some, if not all, of the high-level managers of the acquired firm with existing or newly hired managers of the acquiring firm. Due to cultural differences, both at the firm and national levels, the formation of a new management team involves risk. In fact, as is discussed in Chapter 13, a great number of mergers and acquisitions fail because the acquiring companies are not able to successfully deal with management risk.

2. Legal risks:
   Operating in a new country, especially a country with vast legal differences from the home country's legal system is risky. Some countries' legal system might be based on common law, such as the Anglo-American legal tradition. Other countries, such as China, for

example, might have a civil law system.[2] The variations in the legal systems could create risky conditions in the event of legal disputes. Regardless of the differences among the legal systems of the countries of acquiring and acquired firms, the enforcement of existing laws in the host country might also pose some risk. As an example, in spite of existence of intellectual property laws in some emerging economies, issues from a lack of enforcement of the existing the laws in many emerging economies do arise.

3. Taxation risks:

Countries have different tax policies and tax systems. In some emerging economies, tax incentives, tax holidays, and tax rebates vary according to industries and localities. The variance of tax systems could pose some risk.

4. Distribution risks:

In some merging economies, the distribution of products could pose major risks. These risks arise from the enforcement of contracts. Manufacturers of products supply goods to the distributor on credit, and receive payments only after a certain time period. The manufacturer must make sure that the distributor has the ability to market the products according to acceptable industry standards and terms of contract between the manufacturer and the distributor.

5. Foreign exchange and repatriation risks:

Foreign exchange risk arises because of fluctuations in foreign exchange rates. A party to an international business transaction that accepts the terms of settlement in a foreign currency is exposed to transaction risks. Companies that have accounts receivable denominated in a foreign currency face risk of the host country's currency depreciation. Companies that have accounts payable denominated in a foreign currency face high risk if the home currency depreciates.[3] By the same token, repatriation of the financial assets involves risk of home country's currency appreciation (host country's currency depreciation).

6. Political risks:

Political risks arise when a foreign company suffers losses or does not meet its profit expectations because of adverse political decisions, conditions, or events in the country where the business entity is operating. Notable examples of political risk occurred in Libya. China Railway Construction Corporation had three contracts from the Libyan government for construction of railways for $4.237 billion. All projects had to be shut down after the war broke out in that country in 2011. Also, China State Construction Engineering Corporation (CSCEC), the largest construction firm in the world, had to terminate its operations in Libya after investment of RMB17.6 billion (approximately $2.94 billion), after the start of hostilities in Libya. Moreover, CSCECC had to end the construction of a housing complex with 7,300 apartment units with a contract value of RMB5.54 billion or a little less than $1 billion (Wang 2013).

Types of Mergers

Horizontal Mergers

A horizontal merger takes place between two firms that operate and compete in the same kind of business activities. For example, the merger of two auto firms is a horizontal merger.

Industry roll-ups often involve the horizontal merger of small firms with similar operations.

Vertical Mergers

Vertical mergers take place when firms in different stages of production and distribution operations consolidate. For example, if a company that is involved in exploration, extraction, and transportation of petroleum purchases another company that refines and distributes gasoline, a vertical merger has taken place.

Conglomerate Mergers

Conglomerate mergers occur between firms with unrelated business activities. For example, if an auto company acquires a department store, the merger is called a conglomerate merger.

Types of Buyers

Buyers of companies fall into one of two categories: the operator buyer and the investor buyer. The operator buyers buy companies for the purpose of achieving a certain strategic goal and use the target as a complementary unit of existing operations. On the other hand, the investor buyers consider a target enterprise as a profitable investment opportunity, and acquire it with the aim of selling the enterprise at a profit later.

Differences Between Domestic and Cross-Border M&As

Domestic M&As and cross-border M&As share a number of attributes. However, they are not identical business activities and a number of differences exist between them. The following risks are associated with cross-border M&As, which are not present in domestic M&As (Angwin 2001):

1. The acquiring firms may secure funds in one market for investment in another one.
2. The cross-border acquirer faces exchange rate risks.
3. The acquiring company faces uncertainty resulting from changes in the host country's policies with respect to cross-country fund transfers, taxes, and business regulations.
4. The acquiring firm faces political and economic risks in the host country.
5. The acquiring firm faces expropriation risks due to nationalization of private assets by the government of the host country.
6. The acquiring firm has to contend with long-distance management of the acquired firm in the host country.
7. The acquiring firm must deal with a different accounting system in the country of the target firm.
8. The acquirer might face restrictions in outflows of capital imposed by the host country.
9. Managements of both target and acquiring firms face communication difficulties associated with differences in language and culture.

10. The acquiring firm might face legal obstacles in both home and host countries. The legal risk is particularly formidable in the United States because of the rising number of postmerger, mostly frivolous, class action lawsuits by shareholders. See section "Inspection Problems" in Chapters 3 and 15.

11. The acquiring company might face a certain debt–equity ratio that is imposed by the government of the host country.

Summary

In this chapter, we defined a number of terminologies used in corporate restructuring, M&As, and FDI. We also discussed the motives for M&As. Moreover, we examined risks associated with cross-border M&As, elaborated on types of mergers, differentiated between two kinds of buyers of businesses, and listed those features of cross-border M&As that are different than domestic M&As.

CHAPTER 3

An Overview of the Merger and Acquisition Process

Merging with or acquiring another company is a complicated process. To have a clear understanding of the process, the decision maker must have an overview of different phases of the process. In this chapter, we discuss different phases of an acquisition or merging process.

Although there are many ways to organize an acquisition process, a logical way of doing so is to divide such a process into four categories: strategic planning, screening, acquisition, and integration. We discuss each of these categories next.

Strategic (Long-Term) Planning

Planning implies thinking ahead about how to achieve a goal. Successful enterprises must constantly adjust to changes in technology, changes in production processes, changes in product quality and variety, changes in the organization of industry, and changes in the economic environment in which they operate. Adapting to the changing environment requires planning to compete with the competitors by innovation, which implies lowering the cost of production, offering a better product or service, and providing a superior service to customers. In achieving these goals, the strategic planners must answer the question "how do M&A decisions assist the enterprise to compete successfully?"

Of course in strategic planning for growth of a firm, mergers and acquisitions (M&As) is one of the options available to the enterprise. Table 3.1 shows a framework of five alternative approaches for real growth of the firm. These methods include internal changes, financial restructuring, external opportunities, contracting, and restructuring.

Table 3.1 The available approaches for growth of an enterprise

	Method	Alternative routes to growth	
Existing activities of the firm	Internal	Change strategies	
		Change organizational structure	
		Expand geographic markets	
		Expand existing products	
		New product markets	
		Restructure operations	
		Management changes	
	Financial restructuring	Dual class stock	
		Leveraged recapitalization	
		Leveraged buyouts	
		Charge-offs	
		Share repurchases	
	External	Alliances	
		Joint ventures	
		Acquisitions	Divestitures
			Spin-offs
			Equity carve-outs
	Contracting	Licensing	
		Exclusive agreements	
		Franchising	
	Restructuring	Reorganize operations	
		Downsize	
		Revise strategies	
		Reduce costs	
		Increase efficiency	
		Grow revenues	
		Bankruptcy	

Source: Weston, Mitchell, and Mulherin (2004).

The table lays out the options that are available according to different methods for growth. For example, if a firm wishes to grow using
the internal changes, then it has seven available options to choose from:
change strategies, change organization structure, expand geographic markets, expand existing products, supply new products, and restructure

operations; and management changes. By using the financial restructuring method to create growth opportunities, the firm could adopt dual class stock option, leveraged recapitalization, leveraged buyout, charge-off, or share repurchase policy.

Most of the topics in the table are self-explanatory. However, a few terms require elaboration.

"Dual class stock" refers to issuing of two classes of stocks by a company where the stocks in each class differ in terms of voting right of the stockholders and payment of dividend. The charge-off refers to one-time extraordinary expense of a company or a bad-debt expense, both written on a company's income statement. Share repurchase is the purchase of a company's own outstanding stocks from the market. See Chapter 2 for definitions of leveraged recapitalization and leveraged buyouts.

Screening

After developing an acquisition strategy, the acquirer should search and identify a target company. Screening involves application of a set of criteria to the potential target candidates in identifying the most suitable candidate for acquisition. A number of factors should be identified as the primary selection criteria such as industry, and size of the deal, which is determined by the price of the target.

Many acquirers use publicly available databases such as *Disclosure, Dun & Bradstreet, Standard & Poor's Corporate Register, Capital IQ,* and *EDGAR Online.* Moreover, acquiring firms do use investment banks, brokers, and leveraged buyout firms to identify potential candidates for acquisition, by paying a finder fee.

Proper screening targets set the foundation of successful deal execution and subsequent integration of the combined entity.

Acquisition or Execution

This stage of M&A processes involves due diligence, valuation, negotiations, and deal structuring. We will discuss these terms in detail in the following chapters. However, we will give concise definitions for these terms presently.

Due diligence refers to those required activities an investor must undertake to make sure that the target firm will fit the strategy underlying merger or acquisition. *Valuation* of the target company refers to appraisal of the worth of the target firm. *Negotiations* refer to all set of activities that result in identifying, acquiring, and successfully completing merger with or acquisition of a company. *Deal structuring* is an arrangement between the parties in an M&A deal that defines the rights and responsibilities of both parties.

Integration

Integration of two combined business entities is the longest and most challenging stage of M&A. It involves combining strategic, financial, operational, technological, and human capital components of the combined businesses so that the postmerger entity could function smoothly as one unit. Many M&A failures are due to the inability of acquired and acquiring entities to integrate successfully.

Problems Arising During and After Completion of M&As

Studies have shown that most M&As do not fail, if one defines failure as sale and liquidation of the business. However, if failure refers to inability of managers to achieve the goals of merger or acquisition, then the rate of failure is very high. The rate of failure of M&As falls between 70 and 90 percent (Clayton et al. 2011). What are the contributing factors to such a high rate of failure?

Studies have shown that failures can be attributed to problems arising during three phases of M&A: inspection (due diligence), negotiations, and integration (Hopkins 1999). We discuss the potential failures during the three phases next.

Inspection Problems (Due Diligence)

The problem of asymmetric information, referring to the situation in which the managers of the target firm are more knowledgeable about the target in comparison to the management of the acquiring firm, plays an important role in failure of M&As. In most cases, the buyer of a company (or a product) has less information about the target firm (product) than the seller. As a result, the buyer may discover after the completion of the deal, certain information about the target company, which was not apparent before conclusion of the agreement, realizing that the price paid exceeds the true value of the acquired company (product).

To overcome asymmetric information, in-depth due diligence is absolutely necessary. However, in-depth due diligence is very costly and, in many cases, may be infeasible owing to reluctance of the target company to provide requested information.

One of the major after-the-fact unpleasant discoveries is that the target firm may have substantial off-balance sheet liabilities.[1] Often, the intent of off-balance sheet transactions is to show a low debt-to-equity ratio. As examples, we cite, by now famous, cases of large corporate failures of Enron Corporation, an American giant energy trading company, the world's largest, in December 2001; and the Parmalat group of Italy, a world leader in dairy food business in December 2003. Both of these firms through fraudulent accounting practices and off-balance sheet activities, which camouflaged the fundamental weakness of these enterprises, failed after the unlawful practices of the top corporate managers became publicly known. For details of the illegal accounting practices of these firms, which were unlawfully certified by the auditing firms, refer to Chapters 11 (Enron) and 13 (Parmalat) by O'Brien (2005).

The point of the using the aforementioned listed companies as examples is that even in cases where ostensibly all is fine with a target firm, there might be some dreadful, unknown underlying reasons that would make the target not suitable for merger or acquisition. Moreover, an increasing number of postmerger lawsuits by stockholders challenging transactions on grounds of misleading information given by targets have been filed in the courts of the United States in recent years. A study by Cornerstone Research Consulting firm reports that the researchers "…reviewed reports of M&A shareholder litigation in Securities and Exchange Commission (SEC) filings related to acquisitions of U.S. public companies valued over $100 million and announced in 2010 or 2011. We found that almost every acquisition of that size elicited multiple lawsuits, which were filed shortly after the deal's announcement and often settled before the deal's closing. Only a small fraction of these lawsuits resulted in payments to shareholders; the majority settled for additional disclosures or, less frequently, changes in merger terms, such as deal protection provisions" (Daines and Koumrian 2012, 1).[2] These lawsuits make careful inspection of the target companies compelling.

One approach that many entities use to acquire in-depth knowledge of the target company is an initial purchase of a large percentage; say 30 percent of the target firm simply to test the waters. As an example of such a defensive measure, we cite the merger of Renault and Nissan, when initially Renault, a French state owned enterprise, purchased 35 percent interest in Nissan before acquiring the entire company.

Negotiation Problems

Negotiations, in general, and cross-border negotiations, in particular, are very complex processes. The high complexity of cross-border negotiations that often leads to emergence of problems during its progress arises from differences in accounting, regulatory, taxation, and corporate governance systems of countries of acquiring and target companies. We use the differences between Anglo-American corporate governance laws and Germany's corporate governance to illustrate how the differences in the laws could pose problems in M&A transactions.

Corporate governance laws in Germany require that each publicly traded company with 2,000 or more employees have a supervisory board with 50 percent of its members elected by stockholders and the other 50 percent by the workers (McCann 2005). Usually, this arrangement means that any mergers, acquisitions, or restructurings that would result in worker layoffs would be blocked by the supervisory board. Furthermore, as an antitakeover defensive measure, German corporate laws allow firms to add to their constitution, limits to the voting power of any shareholder to a maximum of 5 percent of the total outstanding shares, regardless of the percentage of share held by any one shareholder. In these situations, the negotiating team must overcome these problems.

Articulating the implication of corporate governance laws in Germany for decision makers in the acquisition of targets in that country is straightforward. Acquiring a company in Germany to capture synergies by layoff of excess workers would pose major postmerger integration and legal difficulties.

Integration Problem

Finally, problems at the integration phase of a merger or acquisition are considered to be the major factors for the failure of M&As. We will discuss the issues related to postmerger integration in depth in Chapter 13; however, here it suffices to say that poor planning; poor execution; or the pace of integration, whether it is taking place too fast or too slow, are the major causes of failures.

Summary

This chapter gave an overview of M&A processes by discussing four stages of the M&A process, that is, strategic planning; screening; negotiation, acquisition, execution; and integration. The chapter also enumerated the alternative methods that are usually available for the growth of enterprises. Furthermore, the main problems that often arise during negotiations and after completion of M&A transactions, which usually lead to a high rate of failure of M&A deals, were briefly reviewed.

CHAPTER 4

Merger and Acquisition Strategy Development

Enterprises operate in evolving, complex environments, and to survive they must change their strategic plans. Strategies provide frameworks for firms on how to cope with and adjust operations to survive and prosper in the changing environment. Strategies are important determinants of the future of enterprises, and are used in the formulation of visions, objectives, policies, and cultures of organizations.

Development of strategies requires planning processes, which should include all members of the organization, even though the chief executive or chief executive group in charge of strategy development must be responsible and accountable for the outcome of the strategic planning.

Developing strategies requires knowledge of the terminologies used in the literature of development of strategies. We define these terms next.

1. **Strategy**: A strategy determines the goals of an organization. Furthermore, strategies define the visions, plans, policies, and cultures of an organization over the long run. Strategies must be reformulated over time.
2. **Vision:** A vision explains why the organization exists and where it wants to go.
3. **Goals**: Goals are broad, long-term results the organization wishes to achieve. For example, a goal of strategy in cross-border acquisition might be the firm's desire to acquire capabilities and resources to achieve sustainable, competitive advantage.
4. **Objectives**: Objectives are short-term, specific steps the organization needs to implement to achieve the goals.

5. **Competitive advantage**: Competitive advantage implies that a firm is able to achieve value growth (sales or profit) above the average firm in its product or service market. Competitive advantage can occur in cost structure, product offerings, distribution network, and customer services. For example, Southwest Airlines uses its airplane fleet 11.5 hours per day compared to an average of 8.6 hours by other airlines in the United States.

6. **Corporate or organizational culture:** Many definitions for culture, in general, and corporate culture, in particular, exist; however, a common definition for the term refers to a set of shared assumptions, beliefs, and understanding among the members of an organization, or in a broader societal sense, among members of a community. An economic definition for organizational culture provided by Arrow (1974) is very concise. Arrow defined culture as a collection of "codes" developed by organizations in their coordination activities.

Building on Arrow's definition, which is based on the notion of economic coordination as a set of "pleasing activities," Cremer (1993) defines culture as "the part of the stock of knowledge that is shared by a substantial portion of the employees of the firm, but not by the general population from which they are drawn" (Cremer 1993, 354).

The monolithic view in defining culture, which is implicit in the aforementioned definitions, should not lead into the belief that corporations or societies have a single culture. In industrial settings, many firms have several subcultures according to occupational, functional, product, or geographic lines that influence the behaviors of the employees (Nahavandi and Malekzadeh 1986).

Cultures evolve endogenously through joint experiences of the members of the community, either organizational or national, over a long time. The shared experiences (process of socialization and passing on the traditions) increase common understanding among the members of the community and in organizations, either private or public, and are helpful in coordination activities of the firm.

Choosing Strategic Objectives

It is a widely held view that M&A activities of a firm should be based on the company's overall strategic plans. Companies can select from a number of strategic objectives through M&A including:

- **Growth**
  The growth strategy could be achieved by increasing revenue, increasing profit, or by reducing the cost of production (achieving economies of scale).
- **Employing workers with the necessary skills**
  Employing skilled and talented employees to remain competitive is another objective of M&A.
- **Collection of a set of businesses that complement each other**
  The aim of such a collection of complementary businesses is to maximize existing or evolving capabilities, and to reduce risk.
- **Defensive action**
  To preempt potential takeover attempts by acquiring companies or to resolve the existing business problems.
- **Take advantage of opportunities**
  To capitalize on unique opportunities that have emerged.
- **Globalization**
  To expand market share abroad, acquire new technologies, and gain marketing capabilities abroad.

Additionally, many M&As are opportunistic decisions based on particular circumstances and needs of the acquiring and target companies. For example, in the cross-border acquisition deal between French car company Renault and Japanese automobile firm Nissan in 1999, Renault's motivations were long term and Nissan's were short term. The market, technological, and financial conditions for Renault were sound. Renault's focus was to have a global partner. However, Nissan faced high debt, was unable to generate profit, and had experienced a decade-long decline in market share (Emerson 2001). In short, one can find myriad reasons for M&A among companies.

How to Develop M&A Strategy

To choose an M&A strategy, a planner should consider the following factors:

- Make versus buy consideration
  Which option is most beneficial: producing the good or service internally or outsourcing?
- Regulatory challenges
  Would the proposed acquisition or merger be blocked by regulatory authorities?
- Competitive environment
  What is the structure of industry of the target firm? Is it relatively competitive or do rival firms with a great deal of market power exist in the industry?
- Availability of capital
  How the proposed M&A is to be financed? Is raising capital to finance the acquisition a challenging proposition?
- Barriers to entry
  What are the barriers to entry? Do legal barriers such as patents or regulatory requirements, or marketing barriers such as massive advertising expenditure in the target company's industry exist?
- Cultural obstacles
  Understanding the cultural distances, both at the firm and in cross-border M&A cases in broader societal levels is of paramount importance. However, even though many business executives believe cultural fit is important for successful, that is, value-enhancing mergers and acquisitions, an overwhelming majority of them believe that culture is difficult to define (Engert et al. 2010). Given the importance of cultural fit for successful M&A, the cultural distances must be critically reviewed in the development of the strategy for M&A. See Chapter 13 for further discussions of the role of cultural distance in successful M&As.

Corporate Development Office, M&A Strategy Development, and Target Acquisitions

Many acquiring companies rely on their corporate development office (CDO) for most if not all M&A and restructuring activities. The corporate development teams are involved in the planning and execution of strategies to achieve organizational goals. The activities of corporate development planners include recruitment of a new management team, entry or exit from certain markets, identification and selection of targets for acquisition or merger, formation of strategic alliances, securing financing, spin-offs of assets or divisions, and increasing intellectual property rights of the organization.

According to a 2011 survey of more than 200 executives from major global companies, 87 percent of CDOs led and 52 percent performed investing activities (Ernst & Young 2011). The lion's share of these activities involves different phases of M&A, which included acquisitions and forming alliances, planning and structuring transactions to maximize stakeholder returns, focusing on due diligence to mitigate risk and drive value, valuing assets, and cost- and tax-efficient deal structuring. When CDO team members were questioned about deal satisfaction, about one-third of the respondents indicated that they were not satisfied about the efficiency of due diligence processes. The survey also found that the key areas in which the CDOs seek outside help are financial, legal, tax due diligence, and tax structuring (Ernst & Young 2011).

Given the complexity and extensiveness of due diligence, many acquiring firms are inclined to relegate at least part of the due diligence activities to outside advisers such as law firms, accounting firms, investment banks, and consulting firms. Studies have shown that the choice of outside advisers varies according to the national cultures of the executives of the acquiring firms (Angwin 2001). For example, the French rely on top corporate executives to contact commercial banks in searching for targets, while the businesses in the United Kingdom rely heavily on commercial banks and accounting firms to identify targets. The Germans put heavy emphasis on their staff, and in the Nordic countries, businesses use a variety of approaches in finding target firms. Moreover, business executives from different European countries who were interviewed about identifying those aspects of outside due diligence that contribute the most in value-enhancing M&A deals had attributed different values to the due diligence areas. However, all of them ranked due diligence, ensuring that the target firm has no substantial unwarranted liabilities, the highest.

Lead Advisers in M&As

The Ernst & Young's survey results point to the challenges corporate executives (lead advisers) face in developing and implementing the M&A strategies. The results also imply that M&As are complicated undertakings that require expertise in a variety of subjects such as law, accounting, finance, and economics. Accordingly, a team of professionals who are experts in these subjects must be organized to lead in the earlier M&A processes such as strategy development, target screening, transaction implementation, and postmerger integration. The main tasks of the team should be to prioritize among the opportunities and challenges, to harmonize strategic and financial objectives with corporate missions, and to manage the M&A process. Specifically, lead advisers are responsible for implementing the following responsibilities:

- Developing the appropriate M&A strategy
- Leading the implementation of the strategy
- Closing the deal within a reasonable time frame
- Helping in appointment of other supporting advisers and experts as needs arise
- Involving staffs of information technology and human resource departments in the early stage of M&A activities for smooth postmerger functional, departmental, and cultural integration

Table 4.1 shows the roles and responsibilities of lead advisers in M&A processes.

As stated in Table 4.1, the lead M&A adviser is responsible for advising in three key areas in any M&As. These areas include legal, accounting, and valuing the target firm. In subsequent chapters, we will discuss many of the tasks listed in Table 4.1.

Table 4.1 The roles and responsibilities of lead advisers in M&A processes

Type of adviser	Roles and responsibilities
Legal	• Draft legal documents such as letter of intent, sales and purchase agreement, share subscription agreement, shareholder agreement, and other documents • Review all legal documents • Assist in implementing all legal procedures including convening shareholders' meeting if the target firm is a listed company • Conduct legal due diligence on the target company • Assist in obtaining government approvals for acquisition of the target firm
Accounting	• Analyze earnings and assets of the target firm • Analyze the exposure of the target firm to debt, liabilities, and contingencies • Review contracts and agreements, which might have financial implications on the potential transactions • Evaluate target company's forecasts • Assess the impact of the acquisition on acquiring company's financial statement by close examination of cost of acquisition, purchase price allocation, pro forma valuation of intangibles, goodwill, accretion or dilution of earnings per share • Assist in determining purchase price for inclusion in the sales and purchase agreement • Determine the tax implications of the deal • Determine the transaction costs • Recommend tax-saving deal structures and financing alternatives • Analyze the impact of postacquisition and suggest efficient integration or restricting steps
Value assessor	Assess the value of tangible assets such as property, machinery, and real estate

Source: Deloitte (2011).

Challenges

M&As also involve challenges that must be resolved by the lead advisers. These challenges include:

- Inability to find appropriate acquisition targets
  Finding a suitable target for acquisition is often a challenging task. Accordingly, many firms in search of an acquisition rely

on a *finder* or *broker* to find a suitable target firm. A finder does not represent either party to a transaction, while a broker acts as a legal fiduciary that represents one side of the transaction, generally the seller. The broker is legally bound to protect the interest of the party it represents. The recommendations for target firms by finders or brokers may not be suitable for the acquiring company. Moreover, recommendation of a suitable target does not necessarily imply further negotiation will take place due to the following factors.

- Inaccessibility of the selected targets due to the lack of interest on the part of the target firms to be acquired
- Inaccessibility of the target because of the target's perception that the acquisition is an attempt at hostile takeover
- Insufficiency of information supplied by the management of the target about the target company so that no reasonable offer can be made by the acquiring company
- Inordinate price request for the target firm by the management of the target company

Summary

After defining certain terminologies used in corporate M&A strategy development, the chapter discussed objectives that are considered in the implementation of M&A strategy. Moreover, it discussed the factors, which are often considered in M&A strategic planning, and examined the important role a corporate development team plays in M&A activities. Finally, the role and challenges of lead advisers in M&A were reviewed.

CHAPTER 5

Selecting a Potential Target Company for Acquisition

As was discussed in Chapter 4, the search for and screening of a potential target candidate require applying a set of criteria such as the industry of the target firm and size of the deal. Of course, the size of the transaction is determined by the price of the target company.

Specifically, selecting a target company for mergers and acquisitions (M&As) involves implementing the following tasks.

Identifying and Understanding the Industry of Target Company

In goal-oriented acquisitions, which seek to fulfill the strategic plan of the acquiring firm, identification of the industry for acquisition has already taken place by formulating the strategy.

To understand an industry, however, one should have knowledge of the competitors and degree of competition in the market. A popular method of measuring degree of concentration in industries is Herfindahl–Hirschman index (*HHI*).

HHI measures the degree of competition in an industry and is the sum of squares of market shares of the firms in an industry. Formally, we express *HHI* as follows:

$$HHI = \sum_{i=1}^{n} S_i^2$$

where S_i denotes the market share of the ith firm in the industry, and n is the number of firms in the industry.

We use an example to illustrate the meaning of *HHI*. Suppose an industry is dominated by a single seller, that is, the company is a monopoly. This implies that the monopoly has 100 percent of the industry's sales. Using the *HHI* formula we have $HHI = S_1^2 = 100^2 = 10,000$.

This means that degree of concentration in the industry is 100 percent, or there is no competition in the industry.

Now suppose the industry consists of 100 firms and each firm has 1 percent of the total sales of the market. Again using the *HHI* formula we have

$$HHI = \sum_{i=1}^{n} S_1^2 + S_2^2 + ... + S_{100}^2 = 1^2 + 1^2 + \cdots + 1^2 = 100.$$

This number is the lower bound of concentration measure in this example and implies no concentration. Therefore, the value of *HHI* in this example falls in the interval $100 \leq HHI \leq 10,000$. Note that in an industry with 1000 firms where each firm has one tenth of the market share,

$$HHI = \sum_{i=1}^{1000} S_i^2 = (0.1)^2 (1000) = 1.$$

This implies that the maximum upper bound for the index cannot exceed 10,000, the lower bound does not assume a fixed number and varieties according to the market shares and number of the firms in the industry. In general, the higher the value of *HHI*, the higher the degree of concentration in the industry.

Assessing the Market Size and Growth Potential

Market share refers to the company's total sales as a percentage of total sales by all companies in the industry. One could purchase market share data from vendors such as Market Share Reporter, Global Market Information Database, and Mintel Market Research Reports.

Of course, having some measure of concentration in an industry is useful in knowing the competitors in the industry and assessing the potential for growth based on reality of the market. For example, an acquirer might merge with a target to achieve economies of scale and increase its market power in an industry with a large number of competitors and firms with little market power.[1]

Appraising the Technological Changes and Trends in the Industry

Appraising technological changes requires an intimate knowledge of the prevailing technologies in the industry. The task must be performed by employees with technical expertise in the technological fields. It is argued that one reason for the development of research and development (R&D) departments by large companies is monitoring technological opportunities and threats faced by them (Mowery 1990).

Identifying Barriers to Entry in the Industry

Barriers to entry into an industry could be formidable in industries with low competition. Barriers to entry include economies of scale, patents, copyrights, licenses, control of inputs, brand royalties, and high cost for consumers to change their supplier. The barriers to entry should be identified during the selection process.

After the selection of an industry based on the aforementioned factors, a preliminary research for identification of a target company in the industry must be conducted. This task requires that the acquiring company develop the acquisition candidate pool.

Developing the Acquisition Candidate Pool

This step of the process should be based on the following:

- Assessing competitive position of the firms within the selected industry:
  As discussed previously, one could use *HHI* in assessing degree of competition in the industry of the target firm.
- Estimation of revenue and size of the firms:
  One could use annual revenues, asset value, or number of employees of the target in determining the size of the firm.
- Market capitalization:
  Market capitalization refers to the total value of a company's outstanding shares. Of course, the value varies according to the price of the stocks.
- Location of operations:
  Location of operations especially in cross-border acquisitions should be identified.

Target Screening Process

The target screening process involves developing target profiles, defining screening criteria, and prioritizing targets. We discuss these tasks next.

Developing Target Profiles

In developing profiles of the target companies, one should keep the following considerations in mind:

- Business strategy (What is the target company's business strategy?)
- List of products sold by the target
- Major news about the firm
- Customer data
- Target firm's consolidated financial data
- Regional and international performance data of the target firm
- Cultural assessment
- Organizational assessment
- Integration options: absorb, maintain separate identity or operations, and partially absorb
- List of subsidiaries, affiliates, properties, directors, and executives
- Based on these considerations, select a number of target candidates from the larger list of target companies.

Defining Screening Criteria

The criteria used for screening should be based on the M&A strategic plan, financial plan, budget, and resource requirements, and should include the following items:

- Affordable price range (how much the acquirer can afford to invest in purchasing the target)
- Target size preference (determine the size of the potential target by market capitalization, revenues, net asset value, and so on)

- Profitability requirements (estimate earnings before interest, taxes, depreciation, and amortization [EBITDA or EBIT], net margin, and free cash flow requirements)
- Determine the desired level of control over the target
- State preference for transaction structure (acquisition of shares vs. assets and acquisition vehicle inside or outside of acquiring company's home country)
- Management requirements (decide on leadership style, expertise needs, receptivity to change, compatibility of culture, and model of postmerger management)
- Define marketing factors such as product lines, customer base, brand reputation, geographic presence, and distribution channels
- Identify R&D requirements such as licenses, patents, R&D centers, and investment
- Examine production requirements such as facilities, labor supply, production methods, and capacity

Prioritizing the Targets

After screening the targets they should be ranked so that the highest ranked firm is approached for acquisition or merger talks.

Financial Assessment of the Acquiring Company

After identification of a target industry or firm, the acquiring company should evaluate its own value before further pursuit of the target. The self-financial assessment enables the acquiring firm to determine its own financial strength and learn whether it has the capacity to absorb another entity. The acquiring company should assess its working capital and capital investment requirements through cash flow projection.

The following important questions must be answered.

1. What is the total financing requirement of acquiring the target and continuing future operations?

2. Will the cash flow generated by the company pay interest and principal of loan for financing the acquisition?

To answer these questions, we first need to define several terms.

Cash Flow Statement

A statement of cash flows is a financial statement that shows how changes in balance sheet accounts and income affect cash and cash equivalents, and breaks the analysis down to operating, investing, and financing activities (Wikipedia 2014).

Operating Activities Cash Flow

Operating activities cash flow emerges from payment of expenses relating to production, sales, and delivery of products to customer activities as well as collection of payments from the customers.

Investing Activities Cash Flow

Cash flow from investing activities emerges from purchase or sale of a real or financial asset, for example, land, building, machinery, and financial securities.

Financing Activities Cash Flow

Financing activities cash flow emerges from inflow of cash from investors, banks, shareholders, and outflow of cash to shareholders, and interest payment.

Example: A company acquires a target firm. The postmerger financial statements show the following cash flows:

- Sales revenues: $25,000
- Cost of goods sold: $12,000
- Net interest payment: $2,000
- Dividends: $500
- Cost of assets acquired: $8,000
- Wages and salaries: $7,000

A cash flow statement for this company is given in Table 5.1.

Table 5.1 Statement of cash flow: January 1, 2012–December 30, 2012

Cash flow from operations	25,000 – (12,000 + 7,000) = $6,000
Cash flow from investing activities	($8,000)
Cash flow from financing activities	($2,000+500)
Net cash flow	($4,500)

Problem 5.1

Company XYZ has the following cash flow activities during 2012:

Net cash flow from operating Activities: $194,000
Investing activities:
  Land purchase: $70,000
  Building purchase: $200,000
  Equipment purchase: $68,000
Financing activities:
  Dividend payment to shareholders: $18,000
  Issuance of bonds payable: $150,000

Prepare a cash flow statement for the company.

Due Diligence

After identification of the target firm, due diligence activities should take place. As discussed before, due diligence refers to processes in M&As with the aim of assessing the potential risks of proposed transactions by close examination of the past, present, and future (so long as the prediction of future is possible) of the target enterprise. The objectives of comprehensive due diligence are said to be "…an objective examination of the target company's financial stability and adequacy of its cash flow, its products and services, the way that the company makes and losses money, the future market, its competitive position, and management's ability to meet strategic objectives. Due diligence should be a comprehensive analysis of the target company's business—its strengths and weaknesses—its strategic and competitive position within its industry" (Angwin 2001, 35).

It is a useful to start due diligence activities by preparing a preliminary information request list. A preliminary information request list follows:

- What are the issues identified in a preliminary assessment of the target?
- What is the financial position of the target enterprise?
- What is known about the background of the potential target firm's management team?
- What is the reputation of the potential target company?
- Are the financial conditions and track record of the potential target firm consistent with the acquiring company's tolerance for risk?
- What is the impact of the regulatory environment on the target firm's future operations?

Often, certain issues arise in due diligence information gathering processes. Some of the typical issues are listed as follows:

- Potential targets are unwilling to supply the requested information for due diligence review.
- Financial statements may be ambiguous or inaccurate due to different accounting principles used in preparing them.
- Much of due diligence information may not exist or may not be available.
- Differences in valuation methods could pose difficulties.
- Nontransferable assets such as licenses may be held by the target company.

Types of Due Diligence

As stated previously, the aim of due diligence processes is to gain an understanding of strength and weaknesses of the target enterprise. In general, due diligence involves two stages: the preliminary stage and the full stage. Full diligence is conducted only after preliminary due diligence warrants further exploration in the processes of acquiring the target firm.

Full diligence, sometimes called confirmatory due diligence, is often outsourced to professional firms such as consulting companies or law firms specializing in M&As after the terms of acquisition have been agreed upon. Due to its specialized activities, full due diligence may be divided into financial, legal, market, technology, and personnel categories. We discuss each of these due diligences next.

Financial Due Diligence

In financial due diligence, accountants take the responsibility of compiling and analyzing the financial data that are supplied by the target firm. The analyses of the data enable the acquiring firm to gain an understanding of the financial conditions of the target company. Furthermore, the accounting analyses would reveal the customer base of the target firm, the main suppliers of the materials to the target, the time frame of the accounts receivable and payable, the risks associated with acquiring the target, the turnover rate of staff, and tax liabilities. Financial due diligence takes the financial data provided by the target to be true, and does not make any statements about the validity of the report it produces, which is based on the data provided by the target firm. The task of validating the data supplied by the target firm is in the purview of an audit firm. However, auditing the target firm is substantially costlier than financial due diligence and takes a much longer time to perform compared to financial due diligence.[2]

Legal Due Diligence

Legal due diligence involves verification of the legal status of the target, validation of licenses held by the target, enumeration and verification of the target's liabilities and assets, and identification of owners of target company's assets. Furthermore, the entity or team conducting legal due diligence advises the acquiring company the legal and business risks of the liabilities of the target. Legal due diligence is often performed by professional law firms or attorneys. To illustrate the potential costs associated with inadequate legal due diligence, we examine the case of Ralls Corporation, a Chinese enterprise, which acquired a wind farms company in the state of Oregon, United States, next.

Case Study: Ralls Corporation and Acquisition of Terna Corporation

In March 2012, Ralls Corporation, a subsidiary of Sany Group, a Chinese company that manufactures wind energy conversion turbines, acquired four wind farms called Butter Creek Projects from Terna Energy USA Holding Corporation (Terna), a Greek company, in the state of Oregon.

In September 2012, U.S. President Barack Obama ordered the Ralls Corporation to divest the wind farm investment, located 200 miles from U.S. Naval Air Station Whidbey Island, Oregon, which Ralls Corporation had acquired in March of the same year (Schlossberg and Laciak 2013).

President Obama's order of divestiture was based on Exon-Florio amendment to the Defense Production Act of 1950 (DPA), which gives the president of the United States the authority to manage domestic industry in the interest of national defense. Title VII, subsection (d) states that "…the President may take such action for such time as the President considers appropriate to suspend or prohibit any covered transaction that threatens to impair the national security of the United States." Furthermore, subsection (e) of the DPA reads "the actions of the President under paragraph (1) of subsection (d) and the findings of the President under paragraph (4) of subsection (d) shall not be subject to judicial review." Subsection (f) of the law gives the President the authority to review the national security implications of foreign direct investments or foreign acquisitions of firms inside the United States by stating that "Factors to be considered for purposes of this section, the President or the President's designee may, taking into account the requirements of national security, consider—….the control of domestic industries and commercial activity by foreign citizens as it affects the capability and capacity of the United States to meet the requirements of national security" (The Defense Production Act of 1950, as Amended 2009, 44–45).

Additionally, the DPA stipulates that "The Committee on Foreign Investment in the United States (CFIUS), established pursuant to Executive Order No. 11858, shall be a multi-agency committee to carry out this section and such other assignments as the President may designate" (The Defense Production Act of 1950, as Amended 2009, 48). The CFIUS is a multiagency committee and is chaired by the U.S. Secretary of Treasury.

The legal problems of Ralls Corporation started with inadequate legal due diligence before its acquisition in Oregon. Having observed the operations of similar foreign-owned green energy companies in the same areas, Ralls and Terna did not notify the U.S. government authorities about the acquisition, believing that they have met all the national security concerns of the U.S. Naval Air Station regarding the restricted airspace of the naval station.

After closing the deal, and 2 months after start of the construction activities, Ralls was notified by the CFIUS, a government agency that oversees foreign investment in the United States, that they should stop construction activities until completion of the investigation of the Ralls energy project. Ralls, however, ignored the notification, having confidence that they have met all the necessary national security requirements of the U.S. government, and further knowing that Sino-American cooperation on green energy development was agreed upon by President Barack Obama and the president of China at the time, Hu Jintao.

On July 25, 2012, CFIUS ordered Ralls to cease all construction and operation activities at the wind farms. Furthermore, CFIUS prohibited all access to the project sites with the exception of those U.S. citizens who were authorized to enter the site by the committee. Ralls Corporation complied and stopped all activities at the sites.

On August 2, 2012, the July order was amended by CFIUS prohibiting Ralls from selling or transferring any products manufactured by Sany to any third party for use at the project sites. Moreover the August order instructed Ralls to avoid selling the acquired company without first obtaining permission from CFIUS to do so.

President Obama's September order of divestiture stated that because of existence of "credible evidence," Ralls "through exercising control might take action that threatens to impair the national security of the United States" (Feldman and Burke 2013). The order gave Ralls 90 days to divest and 14 days to remove all structures and objects from the sites.

On September 12, 2012, Ralls Corporation filed a lawsuit against CFIUS and Timothy Geithner, the then secretary of Treasury, and subsequently amended the lawsuit to include President Obama's order for "unconstitutionally taking property" without due process of law stating that "CFIUS's powers under Section 721 and related executive orders and regulations are limited. It may only review certain 'covered transactions' that could result in foreign control of a person engaged in interstate commerce in the United States. It may not bar a covered transaction from taking place. And, like all agencies, it may not arbitrarily or capriciously render determinations absent any evidence or explanation or by unexpectedly and inexplicably abandoning a prior position or policy, and it may not engage in the unconstitutional deprivation of property absent due process." Moreover the lawsuit claimed that "CFIUS violated the foregoing principles and well-established law when it issued an order subjecting plaintiff Ralls Corporation to draconian obligations in connection with Ralls's acquisition of four small Oregon companies, whose assets consisted solely of windfarm development rights, including land rights to construct the windfarms, power purchase agreements, and necessary government permits. Without identifying any evidence or providing any explanation, CFIUS concluded that the acquisition was a 'covered transaction' subject to its authority and that 'there are national security risks to the United States that arise as a result of' the acquisition. Moreover, rather than propose measures that would have mitigated the purported (yet unidentified) national security risks, CFIUS—again without any evidence or explanation—instead required Ralls immediately to cease all construction and operations and remove all items from the relevant properties; prohibited Ralls from having any access to the properties; and forbade Ralls from selling the properties until all items had been removed, CFIUS was notified of the buyer, and CFIUS did not object to the buyer. CFIUS asserted that these obligations were enforceable via injunctive relief, civil penalties, and criminal penalties" (*Ralls Corporation v. Committee on Foreign Investment in the United States* Document 1 2012, 2).

On February 26, 2013, the U.S. District Court for the District of Columbia, where the Ralls Corporation lawsuit was filed, issued a ruling dismissing Ralls's claims pertaining to the presidential statutory authority to order divestitures, but allowing further judicial review of the claim of unconstitutional violation of property rights of the plaintiffs without due process of law. Citing the defendants' argument that the courts have no jurisdiction to hear cases involving a presidential order according to DPA of 1950, the district court ruled that "The statute is not the least bit ambiguous about the role of the courts: 'The actions of the President...

and the findings of the President... shall not be subject to judicial review' 50 U.S.C. app. § 2170(e). Nonetheless, Ralls asks the Court to find that the President exceeded his statutory authority in imposing the conditions in the order, and that he acted in violation of the Constitution by treating these foreign owners of wind farms differently than foreign owners of other wind farms. This artful legal packaging cannot alter the fact that what plaintiff is urging the Court to do is assess the President's findings on the merits, and that it cannot do. Since the finality provision bars review of the *ultra vires* and equal protection challenges to the President's order, the Court will dismiss those claims for lack of jurisdiction. But plaintiff has also brought a due process claim that raises purely legal questions about the process that was followed in implementing the statute, and that claim will stand. The Court notes that it is not ruling that the due process claim *has* merit—simply that it is bound to go on to *decide* the claim on its merits. The Court will reach that question after further briefing by the parties" (*Ralls Corporation v. Committee on Foreign Investment in the United States* Document 48 2013, 2).

On October 10, 2013, the U.S. District Court Judge ruled on the plaintiffs' claim of failure of the president to follow due process of law in issuing the order to divest, by stating that "Defendants have now filed a motion to dismiss the remaining claim, and that motion has been fully briefed by the parties. Because Ralls has not alleged that it was deprived of a protected interest and because, even if the Court were to find a protected interest, Ralls received sufficient process before the deprivation took place, the Court will grant defendants' motion to dismiss" (*Ralls Corporation v. Committee on Foreign Investment in the United States* Document 58 2013, 2). The ruling was very specific in its reasoning for rejection of Ralls's claim, by stating that "Ralls had the ability to obtain a determination about whether the transaction would have been prohibited before it acquired the property rights allegedly at stake, but it chose not to avail itself of that opportunity, Ralls cannot predicate a due process claim now on the state law rights It acquired when it went ahead and assumed that risk" (*Ralls Corporation v. Committee on Foreign Investment in the United States* Document 58 2013, 8).

Ralls Corporation has appealed both the February and October decisions.

This case is an excellent example that illustrates the dire financial consequences of inadequate legal due diligence, especially in cross-border M&A transactions.

Market Due Diligence

By market due diligence activities, the acquiring company aims to understand the market position, market share, and marketing capability of the target company. The marketing due diligence team usually comprises members from sales, R&D, procurement, and technology areas of the acquiring firm.

Technical Due Diligence

Technical due diligence assumes importance for acquisition of the target company with advanced technology such as information technology, advanced manufacturing, engineering, and emerging technologies. If the acquiring company has expertise in the same technological areas of the target firm an in-house team can conduct due diligence. In cases where the target and acquiring companies have vastly different technologies and operate in different technological fields, outsourcing of technological due diligence and hiring a technology consulting firm are required.

Personnel Due Diligence

The acquiring company aims to gain an understanding of how the key managers and major shareholders of the target company arrived at their current standing through personnel due diligence. The issues of interest in personnel due diligence are determining the educational backgrounds, criminal backgrounds, family relationships, and civil litigation involvements of top executives of the target company. Personnel due diligence is often outsourced and professional background check organizations are employed for preparation of the personnel due diligence report.

Cultural Due Diligence

Culture is an important determinant of organizational effectiveness, especially during organizational transitions that are associated with M&A.

Organizational culture plays a pivotal role in acquisition by exercising profound influence on coordination and control functions during postacquisition integration (Pablo 1994). Reducing cultural differences, both organizational, in cases of domestic acquisitions, and societal in cross-border ones can enhance organizational stability. Accordingly, cultural due diligence in the early stages of acquisitions has dramatic effects on their outcome.

It should be noted that before conduct of due diligence, a *term sheet* be prepared.[3] A term sheet is a memorandum of understanding between the parties that are engaged in cross-border M&A discussions. It stipulates major terms such as valuation of the target, financing mechanism, and other related issues of the business transaction that is to take place. The absence of such a memorandum of understanding between the target and the acquiring firm could result in wasteful expenditure of a large sum of money and substantial time in due diligence and other negotiation activities that are doomed to fail in reaching an agreement.

A term sheet is different than a legal agreement for investment or a sale agreement. The term sheet differs from the latter two agreements for three reasons. First, a term sheet is legally nonbinding. The terms of the initial agreement are subject to change during the negotiation processes as more information becomes available to both parties. Second, a term sheet is written by the financial adviser or the negotiation team in simple language and not by a lawyer in a technical legal format. Third, a term sheet is valid for a specific period, for example, a few weeks, a month, or two months. After expiration of the term sheet, the parties are allowed to negotiate with other interested parties or agree on a new set of terms.

It should be noted that poor planning and inadequate due diligence of governmental policies of the host country, particularly inadequate due diligence in environmental policies and labor market conditions of the host country, could pose major obstacles for successful integration.

To illustrate potential challenges inadequate cross-border acquisitions of enterprises may pose, we cite the example of the China International Trust and Investment Company (CITIC) acquisition of Sino Iron, a multibillion dollar company in the business of extraction of magnetite iron ore in Western Australia.

Case Study: CITIC Group and Investment in Australian Mines

In 2007, CITIC Pacific, a subsidiary of CITIC Group, which is a state-owned financial services enterprise, purchased a mining license to extract two billion tons of magnetite iron ores for 25 years in an isolated region in Western Australia. The mining project was the largest cross-border mining investment of its kind by a Chinese enterprise with 100 percent Chinese ownership.

In October 2008, CITIC Pacific announced a loss of 14.7 billion Hong Kong dollars (roughly $1.9 billion) due to investment in forward contracts to hedge against currency fluctuation. In addition to 1.6 billion Australian dollar initial investment, the operations required an annual investment of at least 1 billion Australian dollars for 25 years of the mining operations.

Initially, CITIC Pacific was to invest $4.2 billion with the starting date of mining operations in the first half of 2009. However, due to a number of setbacks the required investment increased to $5.2 billion and its operations were postponed to early 2011. To prevent CITIC Pacific from bankruptcy, CITIC, the parent company, had to inject $1.5 billion into CITIC Pacific.

What factors contributed to the ill-planned Chinese greenfield investment project in Australia? There were many factors that contributed to the unpleasant situation for CITIC Pacific. These included labor issues; Australian nationalism; a hostile attitude toward Chinese investment in Australia; global oligopolistic control of the iron mining industry by two large mining firms—namely BHP Billiton and Rio Tinto; government regulations pertaining to environmental protection and tax policies; as well as the required large investment in infrastructure such as investment in construction of piers, ports, water and electricity plants, telecommunications, and roads in the barren region where the mines were located.

As an example of labor issues, which emerged because of cultural differences between Chinese and Australians, we note Chinese executives' complaint about the work habits of CITIC Pacific's Australian employees. The Chinese executives of Sino Iron found that "Despite the urgent situation...the local managers still left work at the regular time, took vacations, and expected a bonus at the end of the year. Sometimes engineers would be in the middle of processing concrete when it was time for them to leave, without worrying whether this would cause problems. When there were problems, employees would try to blame each other, and the sense of belonging and loyalty from Chinese firms was nowhere to be found" (Sun et al. 2013, 316).

CITIC Pacific problems were not confined to Australian workers' attitude toward work. Australian nationalism created resentment among many Australian employees of the company. Some workers reasoned that since the company's money belonged to the Chinese government, they need not care for the welfare of the company that has employed them. Moreover, the Australian government had also increased taxes and began regulation of cross-border M&A in Australia. For example, the Australian government announced a 40 percent resource tax on mining firms starting in July 2012.

The Australian environmental protection regulations were costly, and they were stumbling blocks too. For example, per Australian environmental laws the CITIC Pacific "…had monitored the underground water, animals in caves, sea turtles and birds on land, and audited the environmental performance of its contractors in order to ensure the protection of the natural environment" (Sun et al. 2013, 320).

In addition to labor relations, labor costs were also issues. Because of the remote location of mining operations, many mine workers had to come from big Australian cities. High demand and limited supply of labor had pushed the annual salary of an average mine worker to over 100,000 Australian dollars, a sum that is twice as large as the average annual income in Australia or at a level of annual income earned by professors in Australia. Moreover, some workers could take 1 week off for every 3 weeks of work or some workers took 2 weeks off. The workers required the company to pay their airfare so that during their break, they could fly to their homes.

To deal with the high labor cost, the CITIC Pacific management decided to bring in Chinese workers who would perform the same kinds of labor at substantially lower wages to Australia. However, the Australian government refused to issue visa for Chinese workers, requiring that the applicants for work visa to Australia must have a certificate showing their high proficiency in English language (Sun et al. 2013).

This case study clearly demonstrates that without foresight and adequate planning, cross-border investment, either in greenfield form, as was the aforementioned case, or in M&A transaction could face major obstacles in achieving the goals of the acquisition.

Summary

This chapter dealt with target selection processes for M&A. It discussed steps involved in acquisition of candidates and developing target profiles, and defined screening criteria and examined varieties of due diligence: financial, legal, market, technical, personnel, and cultural. As part of target selection, the cash flow statement analysis of a target firm was discussed. Moreover, to illustrate the detrimental effects of inadequate due diligence, two case studies involving a Chinese acquisition in the United States and a greenfield investment in Australia were presented.

CHAPTER 6

Accounting for Mergers and Acquisitions

Accounting for business restructuring is an important step in assessing the financial viability of the proposed changes. In the United States, financial statements relating to any mergers or acquisitions must receive the approval of Securities and Exchange Commission before permit is issued to investors. In this chapter, we will discuss the purchase accounting method, currently the only method in use, for merger and acquisition (M&A) accounting.

Accounting Methods for M&A

Two accounting methods for M&As existed until January 2001. These methods are the pooling-of-interest method and the purchase method. The pooling-of-interest method requires the original "historical cost" of the assets and liabilities of the target company to be carried forward, while the purchase method requires a new historical cost for the assets and liabilities of the target to be specified. Additionally, a difference between the two methods regarding reporting the earnings exists. The pooling-of-interest method requires that the *combined earnings* of the combined businesses for any reporting periods, both before or after merger, be reported. According to the purchase method, the earnings of the acquired company are reported by the acquiring company only after the date of acquisition.[1]

After many years of debate among the concerned parties including investment bankers, corporate leaders, banks, and regulatory agencies about the virtues and weaknesses of the respective methods of accounting for M&As, the Financial Accounting Standards Board (FASB) formed a task force to examine the issue. In January 2001, FASB ruled that the purchase method of accounting for M&As be used. The ruling by FASB to move to the purchase method for merger accounting was based on three considerations. First, FASB argued that the pooling method provides investors with less information. Second, the ruling was based on the notion that the pooling method ignores values exchanged in combination transactions. Finally, the members of FASB's task force believed that the pooling method provides artificial accounting differences, while the purchase method supplied real economic differences.

Beginning in 2001 all companies, which maintain financial statements under International Financial Reporting Standards (IFRS) or Generally Accepted Accounting Principles (GAAP), were required to use the purchase method for business combinations.

Since the pooling method of accounting for mergers is no longer used, we do not discuss the method in this book.

Purchase Method

According to the purchase accounting method, the acquiring company must record the acquired firm at the price it was purchased. All assets and liabilities of the acquired firm must be assigned a percentage of the purchase price of the target firm. This implies that both the assets and liabilities of the acquired firms are imputed according to their current market value. Moreover, the purchase method considers the goodwill that may arise in the transaction as an asset, which can be written off[2] over a 40-year period.

The relationship between the price paid for a target company and the acquired firm's net asset value determines the nature of purchase accounting. Three situations could arise:

1. Price paid = net asset value
   The consolidated balance sheet of the new firm is based on merging the assets and liabilities of acquiring and target companies.
2. Price paid > target company's net asset value
   The asset value must be increased to reflect the paid price.
3. Price paid < target company's net asset value
   The assets must be written down[3] when preparing the consolidated balance sheet.

Example 6.1

Firm A buys another company by exchanging 1 million dollars of stocks for 1 million dollars' worth of assets. The book value of the asset shows a value of $250,000. The acquiring company books show assets valued at $250,000; however, the actual value is $1,000,000. After the merger, the acquiring firm would sell the assets for $1,000,000 realizing an earned income of $750,000.

Example 6.2

To illustrate the purchase method of merger accounting, assume that company A purchases company B. The balance sheets of both companies appear as follows.

$$NAV = A - L,$$

where NAV denotes net asset value, A refers to assets, and L means liabilities.

In purchasing the assets of another company, three situations arise: payment of a price that is exactly equal to, more than, or less than the net asset value. Each situation requires a different accounting procedure. We illustrate these cases next.

1. **Price = net asset value of the acquired firm**
   Consolidate the balance sheets by merging the balance sheets of both companies.

Table 6.1 Balance sheets of Firm A and Firm B

	Firm A	Firm B
Current assets	$50	$25
Fixed assets	$50	$25
Goodwill	0	0
Total assets	$100	$50
Liabilities	$40	$20
Equity (net assets)	$60	$30
Total claims (liabilities + net assets)	$100	$50

Table 6.2 Postmerger balance sheet

	Firm A	Firm B	Consolidated balance sheet
1. Current assets	$50	$25	$75
2. Fixed assets	$50	$25	$75
3. Goodwill	0	0	0
4. Total assets	$100	$50	$150
5. Liabilities	$40	$20	$60
6. E quity (item 4 – item 5)	$60	$30	$90
7. Total claim (item 5 + item 6)	$100	$50	$150

Price paid = $30.

Table 6.3 Postmerger balance sheet

	Firm A	Firm B	Consolidated balance sheet
1. Current assets	$50	$25	$75
2. Fixed assets	$50	$25	$65 A's fixed asset + (firm B's fixed asset – [firm B's equity – price]) $= 50 + [25 - (30 - 20)] = 65$
3. Goodwill	0	0	0
4. Total assets	$100	$50	$140
5. Liabilities	$40	$20	$60
6. Equity (item 4 – item 5)	$60	$30	$80 Firm B's equity is reduced by $10 to account for fixed asset write-off
7. Total claim (item 5 + item 6)	$100	$50	$140

Price paid is less than the net asset value of the acquired firm. Price paid = $20.

Table 6.4 Postmerger balance sheet

	Firm A	Firm B	Consolidated balance sheet
1. Current assets	$50	$25	50 + (25 + 5) = $80
2. Fixed assets	$50	$25	50 + (25 + 5) = $80
3. Goodwill*	0	0	$10
4. Total assets	$100	$50	80 + 80 + 10 = $170
5. Liabilities	$40	$20	$60
6. Equity (item 4 – item 5)	$60	$30	$110
7. Total claim (item 5 + item 6)	$100	$50	$170

Price paid is greater than the net asset value of the acquired firm. Price paid = $50.
*Goodwill refers to the excess price paid for the firm that is above the appraised value of the physical assets purchased.

Assumptions for calculations of figures in Table 6.4

- Both current and fixed asset values are underestimated by five dollars each. The finding is based on the fair market value of the assets.
- Allocate the balance of $10 as a goodwill value.

Income Statement Effects

If after completion of the merger the asset value has increased, which is often the case, the increased asset value must be reflected in depreciation charges.

We illustrate the income statement effects of the write-up[4] of current and fixed assets, under the assumptions of the aforementioned case c.

Table 6.5 Income statement effects of write-up of the current and fixed assets

	Firm A	Firm B	Postmerger: Consolidated income statement
Sales	$100	$50	$150
Operating costs	$72	$36	$109 Cost is increased by $1 to account for higher depreciation because of higher value of assets
Operating income	$28	$14	$41 Income is reduced by $1, because of higher depreciation by $1
Interest (10%)	$4	$2	$6
Taxable income	$24	$12	$35 Taxable income is reduced by $1
Taxes (40%)	$9.6	$4.8	$14 (35×0.4) versus $(36 \times 0.4) = 9.6 + 4.8 = 14.4$
Net income	$14.4	$7.2	$21 = 35 - 14$ Sum of individual earnings before the merger is greater than the earnings of the companies after the merger, that is, $21.6 versus $21
Earnings per share (EPS)	$(14.4/6) = 2.4$ per share for six shares	$(7.2/3) = 2.4$ per share for three shares	$21/9 = 2.33$ One new A share = one B share; A has nine shares after merger

Price > net asset value.

Summary

This chapter briefly discussed the history of accounting for M&A methods in the United States. It further used a set of simple examples of income statements and balance sheets of an acquiring and a target company to illustrate the purchase method of accounting for mergers.

CHAPTER 7

Alternative Approaches to Valuation

This chapter deals with alternative approaches to company valuation for the purpose of merger and acquisition (M&A). Naturally, accurate assessment of the value of the target firm, and determination of the fair price investors should pay for the entity in a competitive market, is critically important for the financial success of the acquisition. However, even though determination of a fair price is the necessary condition for success it is by no means a sufficient condition for eventual success of the combination because a fair price cannot guarantee smooth, successful post-merger integration of the entities.

Several methods for company valuation exist.[1] In this chapter, we examine three approaches that are listed below:

1. Comparable companies approach
2. Comparable transactions approach
3. The spreadsheet approach or the formula approach

We note that there are no analytical differences between the spreadsheet approach and the formula approach. They both use discounted cash flow (DCF) analysis and give the same numerical results. The difference is that while the spreadsheet approach presents financial statements over several years, the formula approach expresses the same data in a compact way in a formula. The spreadsheet approach is more intuitive than the formula approach. We discuss these approaches by using examples next.

Comparable Companies Approach in Company Valuation

This approach uses certain market-based transactions such as market stock price or sales, market stock price or book stock price, and market stock price or net income of comparable companies as a basis for determination of the value of a target company. In the calculation of these ratios, market price of common stocks refers to the price of common stock of the target company after the conclusion of the merger negotiation.

To find comparable companies, one should consider several variables including:

1. Size
2. Similarity of products
3. Age of company
4. Recent trends in sales, and technological innovation

Let us suppose that we found three companies X, Y, and Z that are comparable to the target company A. The data equity value–sales and price–earnings ratios for the comparable companies and their averages are presented in Table 7.1.

We multiply the average ratios by the actual data of the target company A to calculate its current market price. The recent data of the target company A are those that appear in the first column of Table 7.2. We show the results in the third column of Table 7.2.

According to the adjusted equity value, the investors should pay no more than $111 million for the target.

Note that the ratios in Table 7.1 should be close in value and have minimal variance. Otherwise, the companies are not comparable.

Table 7.1 Comparable companies ratios

Ratio	Firm X	Firm Y	Firm Z	Average
Equity (market)/sales	1.3	1.1	0.9	1.1
Equity (book)/sales	1.1	1.2	1.3	1.2
Equity (market)/net income = P/e	20	15	25	20

Table 7.2 *Adjusting target company actual data for valuation based on comparable companies*

Target company actual data	Average market ratios	Adjusted values ($ millions)
Sales = $120	1.1	$132
Equity (book value) = $60	1.2	$72
Net income = $6.4	20	$128
Average		Value of equity of target company = (132 + 72 + 128)/3 = 110.66, or approximately $111 million

Comparable Transactions Method

This method uses the value of some recent comparable *M&A transactions* in valuation of the target company. To illustrate how the method works, we use data from Table 7.1. We assume companies X, Y, and Z were involved in the same type of merger transactions as company A plans to conduct.

Since the postannouncement equity price of a typical targeted company is 30 to 40 percent above the company's equity price before the announcement of takeover, one should adjust the values in the aforementioned Table 7.1 to reflect the price differential. We assume all ratios in Table 7.1 have increased by 0.3, which reflects market valuations after the merger announcement. We assume price/earnings (*P/e*) ratios for Company X and Company Y have increased by 5 and the ratio for Company Z has risen by 2. The adjustments appear in Table 7.3.

Based on adjusted values from Table 7.2 and Table 7.4, we calculate a 15.3 percent $\left(\frac{128}{111} = 1.153 \right)$ premium over the market valuation.

In practice, a bidder would offer the price based on comparable companies model, and then offer a premium over the basic offer during the

Table 7.3 *Comparable transactions ratios*

Ratio	Target A	Target B	Target C	Average
Equity (market)/sales	1.6	1.4	1.2	1.4
Equity (book)/sales	1.4	1.5	1.6	1.5
Equity (market)/net income = P/e	25	20	27	24

Table 7.4 Application of after-merger valuation ratios to Company A

Target company actual data	Average market ratio	Adjusted value of equity
Sales = $100	1.4	140
Equity (book value) = $60	1.5	90
Net income = $6.4	24	153.6
Average		(140 + 90 + 153.6)/3 = 127.87

merger negotiations to reflect the prevailing market prices of the target company's equity after the announcement of the merger.

The Discount Cash Flow Spreadsheet Approach

The DCF spreadsheet method of company valuation involves two steps. First, the analyst projects cash flows of the company of interest into the future, and then uses the logic of capital budgeting for investment decision.

Capital Budgeting

Capital budgeting is an analytical method used in long-term capital investment decision analysis. Capital budgeting analysis consists of comparing the sum of discounted future stream of earnings with the cost of the initial capital investment, which is used to generate future earnings. The method is used in many investment decision analyses including investment in M&A and in valuation of the target company.

Several methods for capital budgeting exist.[2] One approach for capital budgeting is net present value (NPV) calculation. Since free cash flows (FCFs) are used in NPV calculations and capital budgeting analysis, we discuss FCF next.

Free Cash Flows

FCF is the net operating income after deduction of taxes from the initial cost of investment. Formally we present the concept as follows:

$$FCF = \left[X_t (1-T) - I_t \right],$$

where X_t is the net operating income at time t, T denotes the tax rate, and I_t means total investment at time t.

Note 2: Investment rule

$NPV \geq 0 \rightarrow$ Invest; if NPV is positive.

Net Present Formula

The formula for NPV is given below:

$$NPV = \frac{FCF_1}{(1+k)^1} + \frac{FCF_2}{(1+k)^2} + \cdots + \frac{FCF_n}{(1+k)^n} - I_0 = \frac{\sum_{t=1}^{n} FCF_t}{\sum_{t=1}^{n} (1+k)^t} - I_0 \quad (7.1)$$

where FCF_t is the free cash flow at time t, k is the cost of capital, n is the number of years in the investment horizon, and I_0 is the initial investment outlay. Note that the first term on the right side of the equation is called gross present value (GPV).

FCF Calculations

To use Equation 7.1 in NPV estimation of a company is straightforward if we have accurate estimates for FCF and k. We will discuss how to accurately calculate these variables next.

In valuing a company, two definitions of FCFs are used: free cash flows to the firm (FCFF), or enterprise cash flow, and cash flow to equity investors (FCFE) or equity cash flow.

Free cash flow to the firm (enterprise cash flow) is that cash flow that satisfies the total claims of the investors in the company's debt, preferred stocks, and common stocks. FCFF can be calculated using the following formula:

$$FCFF = EBIT(1-T) + DA - GCE - CNWC \quad (7.2)$$

where EBIT denotes earnings before interest and taxes, T is the tax rate, DA is depreciation and amortization, GCE is gross capital expenditures, and $CNWC$ refers to change in net working capital. Also, net working capital = current assets − current liabilities. Note that current assets and liabilities are assets and liabilities that are expected to be realized in a year or within one operating cycle.

This definition excludes cash flows from a firm's financial activities and includes cash flows from operating and investment activities. It is a measure of cash or liquid assets required for day-to-day operations of the firm. In most cases valuation of target firm the concept of the enterprise cash flow is used. Hence, we will focus on the discussion of enterprise cash flows only.

To illustrate how to calculate FCFF, suppose that an acquiring company has developed the financial statement of the target firm, which appears in Table 7.5.

Note that the projected revenue (the data in the first row) started at $1,000 and is expected to grow at 25 percent for 3 years and then

Table 7.5 Projected values for the target company

		Year				
	Percentage of revenue	0	1	2	3	4 to ∞
1. Revenues (R_t)	100	$1000	$1250	$1,562.50	$1,953.0	$1,953.0
2. Costs = (0.8) (R_t)	80		1000	1,250	1,562.5	1,562.5
3. Net operating income (X_t) = (0.2) (R_t)	20		250	312	391	391
4. Taxes (T) = (.4)(X_t)	40		100	125	156	156
5. Net operating income after taxes [$X_t(1-T)$]	12		150	187	235	235
Investment requirements						
6. Net working capital (I_{wt}) = (0.04)(R_t)	4		$50	$62.5	$78	0 *
7. Net property, plant, and equipment (I_{ft})= (0.06)(R_t)	6		75	94	117	0*
8. Total (I_t)	10		125	156.5	195	0
9. Free cash flows [$X_t(1-T)$] − I_t			$25	$31	$40	$235

*Annual investments of I_{wt} and I_{ft} after the end of the third year are 0 because no growth in revenues requires no new investment.

Table 7.6 Valuation of the target company

			Year	
			3	
	1	2	Beginning	End
1. Before-tax cash flow (X_t)	250	312	391	391
2. Taxes at 40% (T)	100	125	156	156
3. After-tax cash flow $[X_t(1-T)]$	150	187	235	235
4. Investment (I_t)	125	156.5	195	0
5. Free cash flow $[X_t(1-T)]-I_t$	25	31	40	235
6. Discount factor	$(1+k)$	$(1+k)^2$	$(1+k)^3$	$(1+k)^3$= exit value*
	1.10	1.21	1.331	10/1.331
7. Present value	$\frac{25}{1.1}\approx 23$	$\frac{31}{1.21}\approx 26$	$\frac{40}{1.331}\approx 30$	$\frac{235}{0.1(1.331)}\approx 1765$
Total value of the target = 23 + 26 + 30 + 1765 = \$1844				

*See this discount factor for discounting of projects with an initial growth and then no growth in Formula 7.3.

experience no growth afterward. The cost is believed to be 80 percent of sales, and to avoid the problem of typing a table with many columns, we assume no capital investments are required after the third year.

Based on the data in Table 7.5, the acquiring company calculates the maximum price (\$1844) it should pay to acquire the target firm if its cost of capital is 10 percent. We illustrate the calculations in Table 7.6.

Formula Approach to Valuation

One can use valuation formulas in valuation of target companies. The valuation formula varies depending on the assumption one makes about the growth of revenues. These formulas are presented in the following page.

The Basic Formula

Assumption: Cash flows grow at a certain constant rate and then will not grow after a certain year.

$$V_0 = R_0[m(1-T)-I]\sum_{t=1}^{n}\frac{(1+g)^t}{(1+k)^t} + \frac{R_0(1+g)^n[m(1-T)]}{k(1+k)^n} \qquad (7.3)$$

Let $1+h = \dfrac{(1+g)}{(1+k)}$; then by algebraic manipulation, Equation 7.3 leads to

$$V_0 = R_0[m(1-T)-I](1+h)\left[\frac{(1+h)^n-1}{h}\right] + \frac{R_0 m(1-T)}{k}(1+h)^n \quad (7.3a)$$

where

V_0 = net discounted cash flows;

R_0 = the initial revenue;

m = net operating income margin;

g = growth rate of revenues;

k = cost of capital;

T = the tax rate;

I = investment as a percentage of revenue;

n = number of years of supernormal growth.

Note that net operating income margin implies a constant growth rate in the net operating income.

The Case of Temporary Supernormal Growth and Then No Growth

Assumption: Sales revenues grow at a supernormal rate first, and then have no growth.

$$V_0 = R_0[m(1-T)-I]\sum_{t=1}^{n}\frac{(1+g)^t}{(1+k)^t} + \frac{R_0(1+g)^n[m(1-T)]}{k(1+k)^n} \qquad (7.4)$$

The Case of Constant Cash Flow Growth

$$V_0 = \frac{R_0(1+g)[m(1-T)-I]}{k-g}, k \succ g \qquad (7.5)$$

No-Growth Case

$$V_0 = \frac{R_0[m(1-T)-I]}{k}, k > g \tag{7.6}$$

The Case of Temporary Supernormal and Then Constant Growth

$$V_0 = R_0[m(1-T)-I_s]\sum_{t=1}^{n}\frac{(1+g_s)^t}{(1+k)^t} + \frac{R_0(1+g_s)^n[m(1-T)-I_c]}{(1+k)^n}\left(\frac{1+g_c}{k-g_c}\right) \tag{7.7}$$

where I_s and g_s are the investment and the growth rate of revenues during the supernormal growth period, respectively, and I_c and g_c are the investment and revenue growth rate during the constant growth period, respectively.

Example 7.1

Calculate the value beyond which you could not pay a target company with the characteristics represented in the data below, if your company is to earn the applicable cost of capital for the acquisition.

$$R_0 = 1000; m = 0.25; T = 0.4; I = 0.1; g = 0.25; k = 0.1; n = 3$$

Solution

Using formula

$$V_0 = R_0[m(1-T)-I](1+h)\left[\frac{(1+h)^n-1}{h}\right] + \frac{R_0m(1-T)}{k}(1+h)^n,$$

where R_0 is the initial revenue, X_0 = m. R_0 is growth in the initial revenue, and m is the constant growth rate in the net operating income (net operating income margin), and the data given in the problem, we have

$$V_0 = 1000[0.2(1-0.4)-0.1](1+0.1363)\left[\frac{(1.1363)^3-1}{0.1363}\right]$$

$$+ \frac{1000(0.2)(1-0.4)}{0.1}(1+0.1363)^3 = 79+1760 = 1838$$

Note that $h = \dfrac{(1+g)}{(1-k)} - 1$.

The firm should not pay more than $1,838 for the target firm.

Note that the valuation according to the formula method and the spreadsheet method should give the same answer. In our example, we do not have the exact valuation number for the two methods. This is due to rounding and approximation of the numbers in Tables 7.5 and 7.6.

Incremental Profit Approach to NPV Calculation

Some analysts use the incremental profit rate, instead of the average profit rate and normalize investment I_t by dividing it by after-tax net operating income, that is, $X_t(1 - T)$. Denote the incremental profit rate as $b = \dfrac{I_t}{X_t(1-T)}$.

Using b and by algebraic manipulation of Equation 7.3, we derive Expression 7.8:

$$V_0 = X_0(1-T)(1-b)\sum_{t=1}^{n}\frac{(1+g)^t}{(1+k)^t} + \frac{X_0(1-T)(1+g)^n}{k(1+k)^n}. \qquad (7.8)$$

As was the case before, we can alternatively use 7.8a:

$$V_0 = X_0(1-T)(1-b)(1+h)\left[\frac{(1+h)^n-1}{h}\right] + \frac{X_0(1-T)}{k}(1+h)^n. \qquad (7.8a)$$

Let us use the data from the aforementioned Example 7.1 and formula 7.8a to calculate NPV V_0.

Note that for the data in Example 7.1, we have $X_0 = m * R_0 =$ $0.2(1000) = \$200.00 \rightarrow$ growth of the initial revenue, $b = \dfrac{I_0}{[m(1-T)]}$ $\rightarrow$ express investment as a percentage of after-tax net operating income.

For this problem, we have $b = \dfrac{0.1}{.2(1-0.4)} = 0.833$.

Inputting the data in Equation 7.8a, we get the following result:

$$V_0 = 200(1-0.4)(1+0.8333)(1+0.1363)\left[\frac{(1+0.1363)^3 -1}{0.1363}\right]$$

$$+\frac{200(1-0.4)}{0.1}(1+0.1363)^3 = (20.004)(1.1363)(3.4274)$$

$$+(1200)(1.46716)=1838.49$$

Note that we come up with the same NPV as before.

Example 7.2

Assume the FCFs for the company in the previous Example 7.1 have no growth. Calculate the value of the company.

Now we use the no-growth formula, which is

$$V_0 = \frac{R_0[m(1-T)]}{k}.$$

Substituting data for the variables, we get

$$V_0 = \frac{1000[0.2(1-0.4)]}{0.1} = 1200.$$

Example 7.3

Now suppose the cash flows for the company in Example 7.1 are constant. Calculate the NPV of the company.

$$V_0 = \frac{R_0(1+g)[m(1-T)-I]}{k-g}$$

$$V_0 = \frac{1000(1+0.25)[0.2(1-0.4)-0.1]}{0.1-0.25} = -166.67$$

Accordingly, given the constant rate of growth in revenue and cost of capital, the NPV of the firm is negative.

Now let us assume $k = 0.30$ $k = .30$. Calculate V_0:

$$V_0 = \frac{1000(1+0.25)[0.2(1-0.4)-0.1]}{0.3-0.25} = 500$$

What are the implications of the results of this example? First, a positive PV requires satisfaction of two conditions: $m(1-T) \prec I$ and $k \prec g$. Second, a positive NPV will be guaranteed if $m(1-T) \succ I$ and $k \succ g$.

Summary

This chapter dealt with the valuation of a company by discussing alternative methods of corporate valuation. Specifically, comparable companies, comparable transactions, and capital budgeting methods were discussed. Moreover, in examining the capital budgeting approach, DCFs and NPV of valuation under different assumptions concerning revenue growth were reviewed.

CHAPTER 8

Cost of Capital

As was discussed in Chapter 7, valuation of a company requires knowledge of the cost of capital. Cost of capital is the opportunity cost a company incurs to secure funds for investment. From an investor's point of view, cost of capital is that rate of return on investment which makes the discounted stream of future earnings equal to the supply price of the asset. This chapter is concerned with the meaning and method of estimating cost of capital.

Estimating cost of capital requires calculation of the components of the cost of capital: equity, debt, and preferred stocks. We discuss the components and methods of calculating them next.

Cost of Equity

To calculate the cost of equity or required rate of return on stock, we use the capital asset pricing model (CAPM). CAPM states that the required rate of return on equity of a firm is determined by the risk-free return and a risk factor. Specifically, we write

$$r_j = r_{RF} + (r_M - r_{RP})\beta_j,$$

where r_j is the required return on stock j,

r_{RF} is the risk-free rate (yield on a Treasury security),

r_M is the required rate of return on all stocks in the market, and

β_j is the beta coefficient of the stock. It measures the risk contribution of the jth stock to the market risk. β is the slope of the line showing the relationship between return on the jth stock, r_j, and market return, r_M. Also, the higher the value of beta, the higher the risk of investment. Note that $(r_M - r_{RP})$ measures the deviation of the risk associated with the market from the risk-free rate of return.

It is important to note that CAPM as previously formulated is a linear function of two variables of the form $y = a + mx$. As such, having the time series for r_j, r_{RF}, and r_M, one could estimate CAPM for any stock and determine β and the vertical intercept. Using the estimated regression model for any given r_M and r_{RF}, one may estimate cost of equity or r_j. For consistency with use of notation in the subsequent analysis, let us use k^e instead of r_j for cost of equity.

To illustrate the concept and application of CAPM, we use several examples.

Example 8.1

What is the cost of equity (required rate of return on stock) for company A, if the risk-free rate is 6 percent, the required return on the market is 13 percent, and Company A's $\beta = 0.7$?

$$r_A = 0.06 + (0.13 - 0.06)(0.7)$$

This means that the cost of equity for this company is 10.9 percent.

Of course, as we will discuss in the following, in estimating CAPM we will use the index for the stock exchange where the individual stock to calculate the rate of returns on all stocks in the market, yields on U.S. Treasury bills as the risk-free rate, and the closing prices of the stock under consideration.

Example 8.2

Using Dow Jones Industrial Average, Citigroup's weekly closing prices, and Treasury bill yields for April 23, 2012 to April 23, 2013, estimate CAPM for the company.

Using the ordinary least square, the estimated model is

$$r_C = -0.001815 + 2.106 ERP,$$

where r_c is investors' required return to invest in Citigroup's stocks (cost of equity), and ERP is the equity risk premium. Note that $\beta = 2.106$ is the risk Citigroup contributes to the risk of the entire stock market where it is listed (Figure 8.1).

Fitted line plot

Rate of return (RC) = -0.001815 + 2.106 Rm-Rf

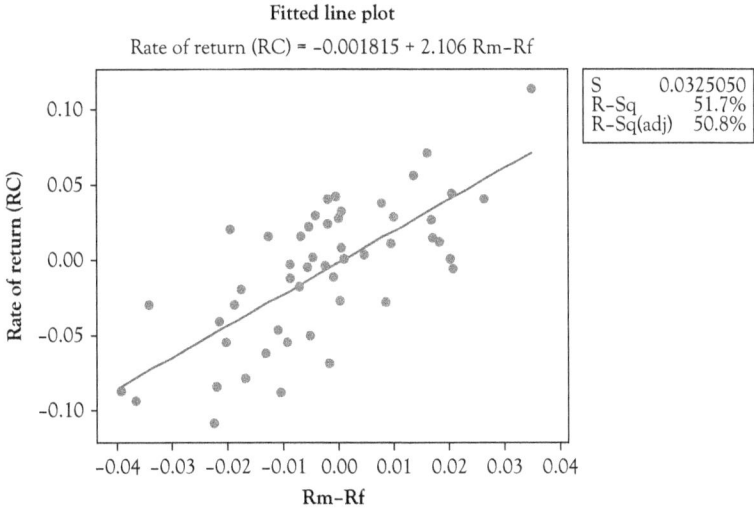

S	0.0325050
R–Sq	51.7%
R–Sq(adj)	50.8%

Figure 8.1 Regression line for CAPM for Citigroup

We use the following values for $r_c = -0.005583$ and $r_M = 0.0213655$ to illustrate calculation of cost of equity for Citigroup on the date with the individual and market returns we are using. According to the estimated CAPM, the cost of equity on that date is $r_c = -0.001815 + 2.106 [0.0213655 - (-0.005583)] = 0.05493$.

It should be noted that the aforementioned estimated model is for illustrative purposes only. Based on the estimated regression when $r_{RF} \succ r_M, r_c \prec 0$. This is, economically speaking, meaningless. In practice, the cost of equity determination is based on long-term historical time series of average returns on equity and yields on long-term government securities. Based on time series observations of returns on equities in the United States between 1928 and 2012, the geometric mean of returns on the S&P 500 stock market index is 9.31 percent, and the geometric average of 10-year government bond yields is 5.11 percent (Damodaran 2014). These numbers imply that the risk factor in the U.S. equity market is 4.2 percent.

Cost of Debt

Another component of cost of capital is cost of debt, which is discussed next. Due to deductibility of interest expenses, we consider cost of debt on an after-tax basis, and define cost of debt as follows:

$$k^d = k_b(1 - T),$$

where k^d denotes after-tax cost of debt, k_b is before-tax cost of debt, and T is the tax rate.

In practice, before-tax cost of debt for a corporation may be calculated by calculating the weighted average of the yields to maturity of all outstanding bonds of the company.

Example 8.3

Calculate the after-tax cost of debt for Company A, given the tax rate of 0.4, and a before-tax cost of debt of 0.1.

$$k^d = 0.1(1 - 0.4) = 0.06.$$

The Cost of Raising Funds via Issuing Preferred Stocks

Approximately, the cost of preferred stocks is equal to the yields on long-term debt. This is due to the common practice of payment of dividend to the preferred stock owners before payment of dividend to the common stock holders. The constant dividend payments for the preferred stocks are another reason for similarity of the cost of preferred stocks and the yield on long-term debt. Moreover, the risk associated with preferred stocks is higher than the risk associated with debt, due to the creditors' standing with respect to their residual claims against the debtor. Accordingly, the cost of raising funds through preferred stocks is higher than the cost of debt financing.

Assuming the dividend payments on preferred stocks in perpetuity, the cost of preferred stock (k^p) is calculated by

$$k^p = \frac{d_p}{PR}, \tag{8.1}$$

where d_p is the dividend per share of preferred stock, and PR the price of the preferred stock.

Example 8.4

Calculate the cost of preferred stock if the price of the preferred stock is $100 and the stock pays $5 dividend at the end of the period.

$$k^P = \frac{5}{100} = 0.05.$$

Cost of Capital as the Weighted Average of Costs of Equity, Debt, and Preferred Stocks

As previously stated, the cost of capital is the expected value (weighted average) of cost of equity, cost of debt, and cost of preferred stocks.

$$k = \omega_1 k^e + \omega_2 k^d + \omega_3 k^P$$
$$\omega_1 + \omega_2 + \omega_3 = 1,$$

where ω_i are percentages of equity, debt, and preferred stock financing of the company, and k^e, k^d, and k^P are cost of equity, cost of debt after taxes, and cost of preferred stocks, respectively.

The Weighted Average

In computing simple average, all observations are considered to contribute equally to the average. For the weighted mean, on the other hand, the observations contribute differently to the average.

The formula for weighted average is

$$\bar{X}_w = \frac{\sum\limits_{i=1}^{n} w_i X_i}{\sum\limits_{i=1}^{n} X_i},$$

where $\bar{X}_w$ is the weighted average, w_i is the weight attached to the ith observation, X_i is the ith observation, and n is the number of observations.

Example 8.5

A company raises capital by selling common stocks, preferred stocks, short-term bonds, and long-term bonds. The size of each category of

Table 8.1 Data for calculation of cost of capital

Capital	Size of capital	Cost of capital	Interest rate
Common stocks	$1,000,000	0.10	–
Preferred stocks	$5,000,000	0.08	–
Short-term bonds	$500,000	–	0.06
Long-term bonds	$3,500,000	–	0.09

capital, the cost of each type of equity, and the interest rates on the short-term and long-term bonds are given in Table 8.1.

Calculate the cost of capital for this firm.

$$\bar{X}_w = \frac{(100000)(0.1) + (5,000,000)(.08) + (500,000)(0.06) + (3,500,000)(0.09)}{10,000,000}$$

$$= \frac{845,000}{1,000,0000} = 0.0845 = 8.45\%$$

Example 8.6

Company A decides to buy Company B. Both companies have a cost of debt of 10 percent and 40 percent debt, respectively. The companies have no preferred stocks. Company A's beta equals 1.2, and Company B's beta is 1.5. It is expected that the beta for the combined company is 1.1.

If the risk-free rate is 6 percent, the equity premium is 5 percent, and the tax rate is 30 percent, calculate the cost of capital for the two firms and the combined firm.

Solution

$$r_{RF} = 0.06 \text{ and } (r_M - r_{RF}) = 0.05$$

$$k_a^e = 0.06 + 1.2(0.05) = 0.12$$

$$k_b^e = 0.06 + 1.5(0.05) = 0.135$$

$$WACC^a = \left(k_a^e\right)(S) + \left(k_a^d\right)(1 - T)(B)$$

$$WACC^a = (0.12)(1 - 0.4) + (0.1)(1 - 0.3)(0.4) = 0.1$$

$$WACC^b = (0.135)(1 - 0.4) + (0.1)(1 - 0.3)(0.4) = 0.109$$

$$k^e_{a+b} = 0.06 + 1.1(0.05) = 0.115$$

$$WACC^{a+b} = (k^e_{a+b})(S) + (k^d_{a+b})(1-T)(B)$$

$$WACC^{a+b} = (0.115)(0.6) + (0.1)(1-0.3)(0.4) = 0.097$$

As a result of synergies generated by the merger, the cost of capital of the combined company has been reduced to 9.7 percent.

Summary

This chapter dealt with cost of capital. Cost of capital is the weighted average of costs of equity, debt, and preferred stocks. We used CAPM as a method for calculating cost of equity. Additionally, we defined weighted average and discussed cost of debt and a formula to calculate the cost of preferred stock.

CHAPTER 9

Real Option Analysis in Valuation of a Company

The discounted cash flow (DCF) approach to target company valuation is based on the implicit assumption that after the investment decision, the decision maker has no options for change. This assumption is unrealistic in that after the investment decision, the management of the acquiring enterprise may have options that could affect the results after the investment. The flexibility in managerial decision making emerges after the acquisition because investment in a new project brings additional new investment opportunities. Accordingly, any investment decision in real assets such as plants, equipment, land, and technology provides *real options*, that is, the right, not obligation, to choose to the decision maker. These valuable options are not captured by the traditional capital budgeting approach in asset or company valuation. These include investment timing option, growth option, abandonment option, and flexibility option. The real option method of valuation of target firm remedies this shortcoming. This chapter deals with real option analysis in corporate mergers and acquisitions (M&As).

The following flow diagram depicts the real options available to the acquiring firm.

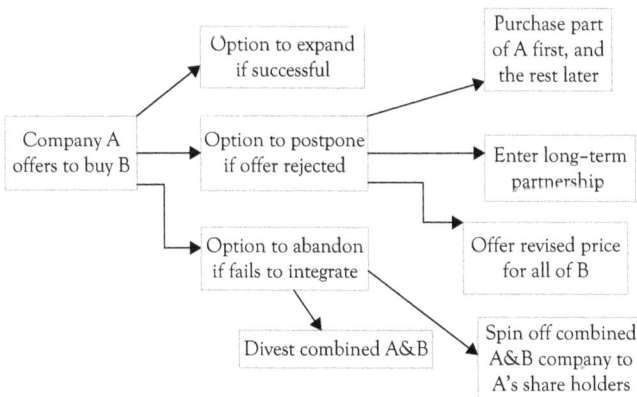

As an example of a real call option to acquire a company, we cite Societa Metallurgica Italiana (SMI) Company's provisional acquisition of Delta, a subsidiary of Finmeccanica, an Italian state owned conglomerate, which was a producer of copper from scraps, not from copper ore, for a modest sum, initially. The option agreement required that the acquiring firm invest heavily in Delta, and in case the firm reached a break-even point after 3 years, acquire it for a previously agreed-on price (Sebenius 1998).

Option Terminologies

It is useful to discuss option terminologies before an analysis of how options are used in M&As.

Options are derivatives, which implies that their values are *derived* from the underlying assets. In general, any derivative contract involves two counterparties. The counterparty that sells the contract is said to be the *writer* of the contract and takes a *short position*. The counterparty that has purchased the same contract is the derivative *holder* and takes a *long position*. The writer of an option receives a premium initially but assumes potential liabilities at a later date.

An *option i*s the right (not the obligation) to buy, sell, or use a property for a specific period for a specific amount of money. An investor who is *long* holder of a *call* option has the right to purchase a unit of underlying asset for a predetermined price at some known time in future, T, which is called the *expiration date*. The predetermined price is called the *exercise* or *strike* price. If the investor is *long* holder of a *put* option, then the same arrangement applies and he or she has the right to sell a number of underlying assets at a certain agreed-on price. An investor who is *short* (writer) in either of the *call* or *put* options has received a premium; however, he or she may be required to buy or sell the underlying assets in future, under the terms of the option contract.

Additional elaboration is useful in comprehending the concepts of call and put options as well as gains and potential liabilities of the writer (seller) and holder (buyer) of the call and put options.

The writer of a call option sells the option to an investor (buyer). What does the investor (buyer) of the call option buy? The holder of the call option buys a legal obligation from the writer of the call option to sell the underlying asset for the call option at the strike price to the holder (buyer) of the option if the buyer requests to do so. The writer of the call option, for receiving a fee, is creating contingent liability against him or herself. By the same reasoning, the writer of a put option, for receiving a premium from the buyer of the put option, creates a contingent liability against him or herself by legally accepting to buy the underlying stocks at the exercise price from the holder of the put option.

We elaborate on the exchanges schematically next.

Schematic view of call and put option transactions

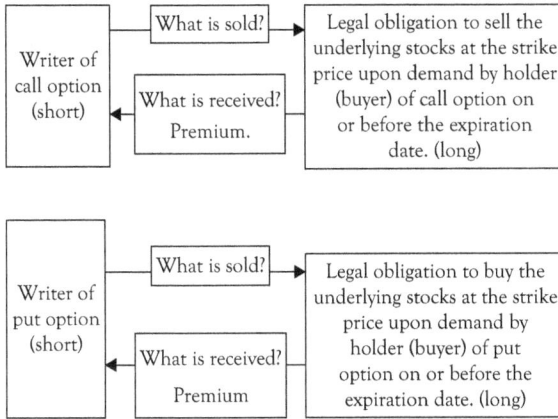

Out-of-Money Options

A *call* option is said to be out-of-money if the strike price is greater than the market price.

In-the-Money Options

A *call* option is said to be in-the-money if the strike price is less than the market price. Buy the item at a lower market price and then immediately exercise the call option by selling it at a higher strike price.

A *put* option is said to be in-the-money if the strike price is higher than the market price. Buy the item at a lower market price and then exercise the option by selling it at the agreed-on higher strike price.

American Option

In an American option, one can exercise the options any time before the option expires.

European Option

A European option can only be exercised on its expiration date.

The Option Premium (Option Price)

The option premium is the price the buyer pays the seller for the rights received by the option contract. It is the price of the option.

Illustration of Mechanics of Working of Call and Put Options

We illustrate the mechanism of how options work by examples.

Call Option

The payoff for a European call option with the underlying asset price S, an expiration date of T, and strike price K, that is, $c(S,T)$ is given as follows:

$$c(S,T) = \max(S - K, 0).$$

This implies that if $K > S$, that is, if the strike price is higher than the prevailing market price of the asset, the option is worthless and the holder will abandon it. We illustrate this concept by an example as follows.

Example 9.1

You believe that XYZ company's stock with a closing price of $20.00 the day before will go up over the next 3 months. You buy the right to purchase 100 shares of XYZ (a call option) at the strike price of $25.00 with the expiration date of 90 days. Suppose the XYZ call option price is $0.50 per share, or a total cost of $(0.5)(100) = \$50.00$ for the option.

Possible Scenarios of the Investment Outcomes

a. At the expiration date, the option is in-the-money (the market price is greater than the strike price). The call option holder will buy at the strike price ($25) and sell at the market price ($35), realizing a profit (see Figure 9.1) of

$$\pi = (100)(35) - (100)(25) - (100)(0.5) = \$50.$$

b. Suppose the market price = $20.00 at the expiration date. You would not exercise the option and simply lose $50.00 (Figure 9.2).

Put Option

The payoff for a European put option with the underlying asset price S and an expiration date of T, that is, $p(S, T)$ is

$$p(S,T) = \max(K - S, 0).$$

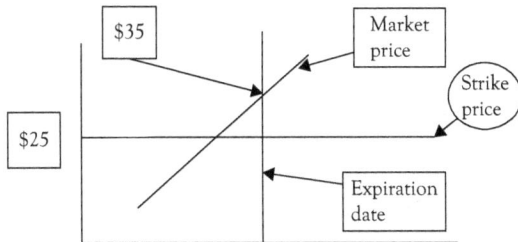

Figure 9.1 Call option in-the-money scenario

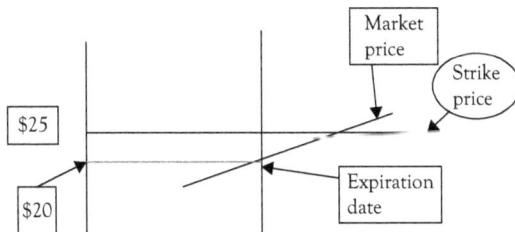

Figure 9.2 Call option out-of-money scenario

Example 9.2

You believe that XYZ company's stock with a closing price of $20.00 the day before will go down over the next 3 months. You buy the right to sell 100 shares of XYZ (a put option) at the strike price of $25.00 with the expiration date of 90 days. Suppose the XYZ put option price is $0.50 per share, or a total cost of (0.5)(100) = $50.00 for the option.

Possible Put Option Scenarios

a. Put option in-the-money scenario:

On the expiration date, the market price is below the strike price. Since you have the right to sell at the strike price, which is higher than the market price, you will purchase 100 shares at $18 per share and immediately sell at the strike price of $25 for a total profit (see Figure 9.3) of

$$\pi = (100)(25) - (100)(18) - (100)(0.5) = \$20.$$

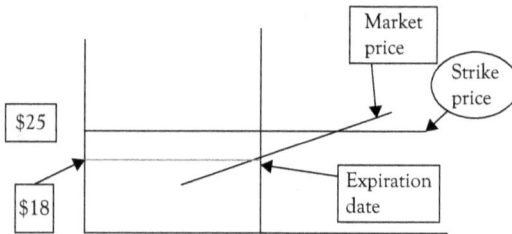

Figure 9.3 Put option in-the-money scenario

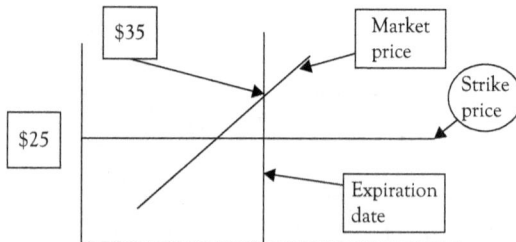

Figure 9.4 Put option out-of-money scenario

b. Put option out-of-money scenario (Figure 9.4):

The strike price of $25 is below the market price of $35. It is not profitable to buy the stocks at $35 per share and then exercise the right to sell for $25. Do not exercise the option.

Types of Options

Two kinds of options exist: Financial options involve financial assets like stocks and currencies, and real options are based on real assets such as land, commercial real estate, equipment, licenses, copyrights, trademarks, and patents.

The motivation to buy or sell a real option is the hope that the agreed price deviates from the market price substantially during the duration of the contract. For example, suppose a firm has an option to lease an office space in downtown Chicago (the lessee) at a predetermined rent. The value of the option increases as the prevailing rent for the office space rises above the agreed-on rent. If the management of the company that wishes to lease the office space believes that rent for office spaces in downtown Chicago will rise, they would enter into a call option contract with the property owner (the lessor), obtaining the *right to lease* and obligating the writer of the call option (the owner of the property or the lessor) to lease the property at the agreed-on rent. The writer of the option is *short* and the holder of the option is *long*.

Of course, risks are ubiquitous in business. On many occasions, the managers of enterprises do not find large investment in a target enterprise prudent, particularly in a new industry or country. Instead of total commitment to invest in such undertaking, they may test the waters by a relatively small investment first and by acquiring the option to expand later when appropriate conditions for further outlays are present.

When merging with a target firm, many outstanding issues facing the target firm could enter as important determinants in valuation of the target company. The acquirer decision on whether to acquire the target might be contingent upon resolution of the outstanding issues. For example, acquisition of a U.S.-based pharmaceutical target firm might be contingent upon the target receiving approval from the Food and Drug Administration, the regulatory agency in the United States in marketing a new drug. Or merging with a target firm might depend on adjudication of a patent dispute or settlement of a lawsuit. These are examples of circumstances that provide *preclosing options* to the acquiring firm.

The management of the acquiring firm is well-advised if they include *postclosing real options* in the agreement also. The postclosing options involve the opportunity to expand, abandon, or postpone acquisition of the target enterprise. For example, the acquiring firm might make additional investment in the target company after closing contingent upon the actual cash flows of the target. If the actual cash flows are less than the anticipated cash flow, the acquirer might delay or abandon the target firm either through divestiture or liquidation. On the other hand, if the actual cash flows are exceeding the expectation, the acquiring enterprise might increase the level of investment in the target company.

Valuing Real Options for M&As[1]

On many occasions, investors have the choice of timing the acquisition of the target firm. The options are immediate investment, no investment, and delayed investment until more information becomes available or more favorable conditions prevail. In the presence of options to investment, the traditional DCF method cannot capture the value of the option present. We use the following examples to illustrate this important point.

Case 1: Expected Cash Flow and Investment Value Without and With Option to Delay Investment. No Initial Capital Outlay

Consider an investor having the option of investing $10,000 in acquiring a target firm or foregoing the acquisition. The acquisition could generate either an annual free cash flow (FCF) of $1,000 or free cash flow of $100, each with the probability $p = 0.05$. The cash flows are expected to remain constant at the first year level and would last until perpetuity. The discount rate is equal to the risk-free rate of 2 percent.

Assumption 1

Invest $10,000.00 in t_0.

Expected value of annual cash flows,

$$E(FCF) = (0.05)(1000) + (0.5)(100) = 550.$$

Expected value of the acquisition, $E = (FCF) = \$550$ at the start of first year of investment:

$$V[E(FCF)] = \frac{550}{0.02} = \$27,500.$$

Note that the expected FCF is to occur at the end of the first year; hence we should discount the value of the expected cash flow at the end of the first year. This means discounting $550 for one year at 2 percent has a discounted value of $27,500 at the start of the year of the discounting.

Net present value of acquisition:

$$NPV = 27,500 - 10,000 = \$17,500.$$

Assumption 2

Delay acquisition for 1 year until uncertainty of FCFs is eliminated. Two situations could arise.

1. Either free cash flow is $FCF = \$100$.

   Value of acquisition: $\frac{100}{0.02} = \$500$. No acquisition will take place.

2. Or free cash flow is

   $FCF = \$1000$.

   Value of acquisition: $\frac{1000}{0.02} = \$50,000$ if

   $NPV = 50,000 - 10,000 = \$40,000$ a year from today.
   Discounted value of acquisition a year from today

   $$= \frac{40000}{1.02} = \$39215.68.$$

Given the probability of 0.5, the NPV of the acquisition with the option to wait is $0.5 \times 39215.68 = \$19,607.84$.

Comparing the NPVs of the acquisition with the option to wait ($19,707.84) or acquisition without the option to wait $(17,500) reflects the value of the real option, which is $2207.

Case 2: Expected Cash Flow and Investment Value With Stages in Investment

A more realistic scenario is a situation when learning about the actual sizes of the expected future cash flows requires an initial investment. Let us use the previous example in case 1 (FCF is either $100 or $1,000, each with the probability of 0.5) but with the requirement that learning about the expected FCF needs some initial investment of $1,250.00 at t_0. Suppose that in addition to the initial investment, the balance of $8,750 will be needed at the start of the second year to generate FCF from the second year onward. Suppose the cost of abandonment of the project is $100.

In such a scenario, the expected net present value $E(NPV)$ of the acquisition is calculated as follows:

$$E(NPV) = (0.5)\left(-1250 - \frac{100}{1.02}\right) + (0.5)\left[(-1250) + \frac{\left(\frac{1000}{0.02} - 8750\right)}{1.02}\right]$$

$NPV = \$18{,}921.6.$

The logic of the formula follows. By assumption, we have equal probabilities of losing, the first term on the right-hand side of the equation, and gaining, the second term on the right-hand side of the equation. The loss consists of initial investment plus the discounted value of $100 abandonment cost. The gain is the discounted value of the sum of the FCF of $1000, which is to occur at the start of the second year and the remaining investment expenditure minus the initial investment outlay ($1,250) at the start of the first year.

In principle, one can continue with such calculations provided that the probability of cash flows and the cost of capital are known. These important parameters are not readily available in reality, however. Instead, many analysts use a more straightforward approach in real option valuation, a method that is known as the Black–Scholes model. We will discuss the Black–Scholes model for valuation of options in Chapter 10.

Summary

This chapter began with the argument that the traditional capital budgeting approach in valuation of companies rests on the notion that after the investment decision, the decision to invest is irreversible and that investors have no choice to alter the decision. In reality, however, investment decisions are not immutable, and several after-the-fact options are available to the investors. This brings option analysis to the forefront of the discussions.

After introducing the meanings of call and put options and other option terminologies, the chapter discussed the mechanisms of in- and out-of-money call and put options. Moreover, the idea of real options was introduced and determination of the value of real options under different scenarios was presented.

CHAPTER 10

Valuation of the Target Company Using the Black–Scholes Model

In the framework of a merger and acquisition (M&A), a real call option gives the acquiring company the right, not the obligation, to acquire the target during the time the call option is valid.

As discussed in Chapter 9, one could use a real call option in valuing a target company. Here we discuss the Black–Scholes model for option pricing by first using an example of an option involving stocks and then by another example that illustrates valuation of a potential target firm.

Black and Scholes (1973) developed a model for pricing the fair value of European options. The model is a partial differential equation, which describes the dynamics of option price adjustment within the time to expiration of the option. The derivation of Black–Scholes option pricing formulas is beyond the scope of the study. It suffices to say that the Black–Scholes stochastic differential equation has the following form:

$$\frac{\partial V}{\partial t} + \frac{1}{2}\sigma^2 S^2 \frac{\partial^2 V}{\partial S^2} + rS\frac{\partial V}{\partial S} - rV = 0, \tag{10.1}$$

where V is the investor's long position in one option, σ is the standard deviation or a measure of volatility of the underlying asset of the option, S is the asset price, t is time, and r is the risk-free interest rate (interest rate on U.S. Treasury bills).

Pricing the option requires that the aforementioned differential equation be solved. However, an analytical closed form solution[1] for some of the stochastic differential equations modeling the dynamics of the option may not exist. For example, American and Asian options[2] do not have analytical, closed form solutions (Richardson 2009). In such cases, one must use one of the numerical methods in solving the differential equations. These numerical methods include finite difference, binomial,[3] and Monte Carlo methods. However, discussions of these techniques are beyond the scope of the present work.

The analytical solutions to the Black–Scholes formulas for European call (c) and put (p) options for nondividend paying stocks are[4]

$$c = SN(d_1) - Xe^{rT}N(d_2) \qquad (10.2)$$

$$p = Xe^{-rT}N(-d_2) - SN(-d_1), \qquad (10.3)$$

where

$$d_1 = \frac{\ln\left(\dfrac{S}{X}\right) + r_F T}{\sigma\sqrt{T}} + \frac{1}{2}\sigma\sqrt{T} \qquad (10.4)$$

$$d_2 = d_1 - \sigma\sqrt{T} \qquad (10.5)$$

The terms in the formula are defined below:

c = European call option price

p = European put option price

S = present value of incremental cash flows (current stock price in call option)

X = investment to create the option (exercise price)

s = volatility of cash inflows (standard deviation of stock price)

T = life of the option

r_F = risk-free interest rate

$N(x)$ = the cumulative probability distribution function for a standard normal distribution. See Figure 10.1.

A number of points concerning the option formulas should be kept in mind. We list these important notes.

Histogram of Z–values
Normal

Mean	0.05566
StDev	0.8907
N	100

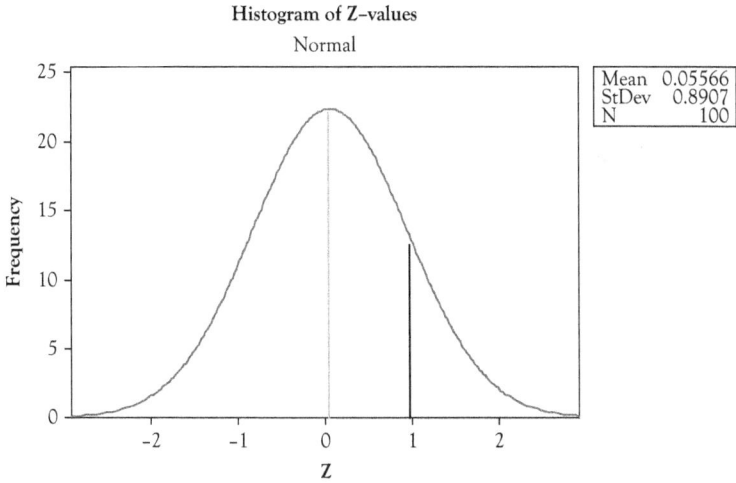

Figure 10.1 A standardized normal distribution

- The standardized normal probability distribution has a mean 0 and a standard deviation of 1.
- $N(x)$ indicates the probability of a random variable assuming a value less than x or its standardised value Z.
- In the preceding graph, the probability of a random variable x ≤ 1 (or its standardized value $Z{\leq}1$) is the area under the curve to the left of the vertical line, where $Z{=}1$.
- The table for $N(x)$ appears in statistical textbooks, or can be calculated by the NORMSDIST function in Excel.
- The value of $N(d)$ falls in the unit interval: $0 \leq N(d) \leq 1$ with $N(-\infty) = 0$, $N(0) = \dfrac{1}{2}$, and $N(+\infty) = 1$.
- Note that because of the symmetric nature of the normal probability distribution, $(1 - N(d)) = N(-d)$.
- The term $N(d_1)$ is the probability of the future value of the underlying asset that is conditional on $S_T \succ X$, where S_T is the asset price at the expiration date. $N(d_2)$ measures the probability that the option will be exercised, which also implies that call option is in-the-money; otherwise, when $S_T \prec X$, the call option would not be exercised.

Calculation of Normal Distribution Using Approximation Method

When one does not have access to a table of area under the curve of a normal distribution or Excel spreadsheet software is not available, one could calculate the cumulative normal distribution function by polynomial approximation to sixth decimal accuracy using the following formula:

$$N(x) = 1 - N'(x)(a_1 k + a_2 k^2 + a_3 k^3 + a_4 k^4 + a_5 k^5) \quad \text{if } x \geq 0 \quad (10.6)$$

and

$$N(x) = 1 - N(-x) \quad \text{if } x \prec 0, \quad (10.7)$$

where $= \dfrac{1}{1 + \gamma x}$; $\gamma = 0.2316419$; $a_1 = 0.31938153$; $a_2 = -0.356563782$; $a_3 = 1.781477937$; $a_4 = -1.821255978$; $a_5 = 1.330274429$; and

$$N'(x) = \frac{e^{\frac{-x^2}{2}}}{\sqrt{2\pi}}. \quad (10.8)$$

Note that the values of the constants γ and a_i, $i = 1,2,\ldots,5$, are given. See Abramowitz and Stegan (1972).

Example 10.1

Let Z = 1. Calculate the area under the normal distribution function for this random variable using the polynomial approximation method.

$$k = \frac{1}{1 + 0.2316419} = 0.811924$$

$$N(1) = 1 - \frac{2.71828^{\frac{-(1)^2}{2}}}{\sqrt{2\pi}} \begin{bmatrix} (0.31938153)(0.811924) - \\ (0.356563782)(0.811924)^2 + \\ (1.781477937)(0.811924)^3 - \\ (1.821255978)(0.811924)^4 + \\ (1.330274429)(0.811924)^5 \end{bmatrix}$$

$$= 0.8413$$

Does the number in the table of areas under the normal curve for $Z = 1$ confirm this value? The answer is yes. The area under the curve or Z from $-\infty$ to 0 equals 0.5 and from 0 to 1 equals 0.34136. Combining the area of the curve from 1 to $-\infty$ gives the value of 0.8413.

Example 10.2

The stock price 6 months from the expiration of an option is $42, the exercise price of the option is $40, the risk-free interest rate is 0.1 per annum, and the volatility is 0.2 per year. Calculate the call option price for this stock.

Solution

The data in the problem are given below:

$$s = 42, \ X = 40, \ r = 0.1, \ \sigma = 1.2, \ T = 0.5$$

$$d_1 = \frac{\ln\left(\dfrac{42}{40}\right) + ((0.1)(0.5))}{0.2\left(\sqrt{0.5}\right)} + \frac{0.2\left(\sqrt{0.5}\right)}{2} = 0.7693,$$

$$d_2 = 0.7693 - 0.2\left(\sqrt{0.5}\right) = 0.6278$$

Next using values for d_1 and d_2, and formula for the call option, we have:
$$C = 42N(0.7693) - 38.049N(0.6278).$$

Note 1: $Xe^{(-r_F T)} = X\left[\dfrac{1}{e^{r_F T}}\right] = 40\left[\dfrac{1}{(2.71)^{(0.1)(0.5)}}\right] = 38.049.$

Note 2: Using a table for standard normal distribution, we get
$N(0.7693) = 0.7791,$
$N(0.6278) = 0.7349,$
$C = (42)(0.7991) - (38.049)(0.7349) = 4.76.$

The stock price must increase $2.76 above its current price of $42, for the purchaser of the call to break even.

Estimating Volatility of the Returns on the Underlying Asset from Historical Data

Another important variable in the Black–Scholes formula to consider is the variance of the rate of return on the underlying asset of the options. This is a measure of volatility of the returns on the underlying asset of the option and measures our uncertainty about the returns on the investment.

To estimate the variance of the rate of the return on the underlying asset, let us suppose that we have n observations in our data set. Let S_i represent the stock price at the end of the ith interval, where $i = 1,2,\ldots,n$. Then let the returns to the stock be u_i such that

$$u_i = \ln\left(\frac{S_i}{S_{i-1}}\right). \qquad (10.9)$$

Let s represent the estimated standard deviation of u_i, so that

$$s = \left[\frac{1}{n-1}\sum_{i=1}^{n}(u-\bar{u})^2\right]^{0.5} = \left[\frac{1}{n-1}\sum_{i=1}^{n}u^2 - \frac{1}{n(n-1)}\left(\sum_{i=1}^{n}u_i\right)\right], \quad (10.10)$$

where $\bar{u}$ is the mean of u_i. Note that $u_i = \ln S_i - \ln S_{i-1}$ approximately measures the rate of change (returns) of the stock price.

Time Variability of Volatility of Financial Time Series

The estimated values of $\bar{u}$ and s in Formula 10.10 are dependent on the time series observations of the stock price. This means that the expected value and variance of the time series are not constant but are time-varying. For example, if we calculate the mean and variance of stock price of Citigroup, for example, for two periods, say daily closing prices for 2012 and for 2013, we will obtain two different volatility measures. Hence, the mean and variance of the stock price time series change over time and show periods of high and low volatility. Moreover, investors are interested in volatility of financial assets for the period they wish to hold the assets, and not for a historical period. Accordingly, note that in the following discussions the volatility of stock prices is time dependent.

Based on assumptions about the returns of the underlying assets of options, Black and Scholes derived the probability distribution of the returns on the underlying assets. First, the Black–Scholes model assumes that asset prices in general (financial asset prices in particular) follow random walk processes. Second, the model assumes that the returns on the underlying asset in a short period signified Δt are normally distributed, and third, it is assumed that the returns on the asset in two nonoverlapping periods are independent. Specifically, this in the discrete time framework, implies that

$$\frac{\Delta S}{S} \sim \phi\left(\mu \Delta t, \sigma^2 \Delta t\right), \tag{10.11}$$

where ΔS is the change in the price of the underlying asset S during a very short time Δt, σ^2 is the variance of the asset price, and μ is the expected return on the asset during time Δt. This implies that the variance of the returns is proportional to Δt.

Note that the fraction on the left side of the expression is the percentage rate of change in the asset price, the term on the right side of the expression represents a normal distribution with $\mu \Delta t$ being the mean of the returns, and $\sigma^2 \Delta t$ representing the variance of the stock price series. Expressing it differently, relationship 10.11 states that the rate of return on an asset is proportional to the mean and variance of the distribution of the asset price observations during the relevant time.

The assumptions leading to the expression 10.11 describing the distribution of asset returns imply that the stock price will have a lognormal distribution at any future period. A lognormal distribution is skewed to the right, where the random variable $S \geq 0$. By logarithmic transformation, we exclude the cases where the stock price could assume a negative value under normal probability distribution. After all, the worst-case scenario for investment in an asset is that its price falls to 0 and the asset becomes worthless.

A random variable with the distribution property, which cannot assume a negative value, has a natural logarithm that is normally distributed. The assumptions of the Black–Scholes model for the asset prices (previously stated) imply that $\ln S_T$ is normal, where S_T is the asset price during any length of time $T = t - t^*$, t is the current time, and t^* is the end of the investment (the time of selling the investment asset) in future.[5] The derivation of the formulas for the mean and standard deviation of $\ln S_T$ is beyond the scope of this book, and they are shown to be $\ln S_0 + \left(\mu - \dfrac{\sigma^2}{2}\right)T$ and $\sigma\sqrt{T}$, respectively, where S_0 is the current stock price (Hull 2011). Moreover, the probability distribution of $\ln S_T$ is written as

$$\ln S_T \sim \phi\left[\ln S_0 + \left(\mu - \frac{\sigma^2}{2}\right)T, \sigma^2 T\right]. \tag{10.12}$$

Accordingly, we could write the standard deviation of u_i based on the historical data, in time τ approximately as $\sigma\sqrt{\tau}$, where τ is the length of time interval in years. Hence we can write

$$\hat{\sigma} = \frac{s}{\sqrt{\tau}}, \tag{10.13}$$

where $\hat{\sigma}$ is an estimate of σ, and τ is the length of time in years.

Note that the value of the standard deviation $\hat{\sigma}$ depends on time τ. As τ increases, the standard deviation of the random variable u_i declines.

Example 10.3

Consider a stock with an annual expected return of 25 percent and a volatility (standard deviation) of 30 percent per year. Calculate the following:

a. The probability distribution of the average rate of return on stock for 6 months
b. The probability distribution of the average rate of return on stock for 4 years

Solution

a. $\mu = 0.25 - \dfrac{0.3^2}{2} = 0.205$, $\sigma = \dfrac{0.30}{\sqrt{\dfrac{6}{12}}} = 0.4242$, $\phi\left(0.205, 0.4242\right)$

b. $\mu = 0.25 - \dfrac{0.3^2}{2} = 0.205,\ \sigma = \dfrac{0.3}{\sqrt{4}} = 0.15,\ \phi(0.205, 0.15)$

As can be seen from the estimated values, the expected rate of return remains constant, but the volatility tends to decrease, the longer the asset is held.

Example 10.4

a. Specify the probability distribution (calculate the mean and standard deviation) of a stock with an initial price of $50, an expected annual return of 20 percent, and a volatility of 15 percent per annum, for a 6-month duration.

b. Construct a 95 percent confidence interval for the stock price for 6 months.

In solving this problem, we first use Formula 10.12. Note that in this example $T = \dfrac{12}{2}$, that is, 6 months.

$$\ln S_T \sim \phi\left[\ln 50 + \left(0.2 - \dfrac{0.15^2}{2}\right)\times 0.5, 0.15\sqrt{0.5}\right]$$

$$\ln S_T \sim \phi(4.0063, 0.106).$$

The knowledge of distribution of a random variable is very useful in practice. For instant, an investor may wish to assess the range of values the price of a stock may vary by determining the maximum and minimum limit of its variation. To achieve this goal, one should construct a confidence interval for the stock price.

To construct a 95 percent confidence interval, we use the central limit theorem, a statistical theorem, which states that 95 percent of the sample means from a population, regardless of the shape of its distribution, falls within 1.96 standard deviations of its mean. This implies that $\mu \pm 1.96\sigma$. Since the estimated mean and standard deviation of the prices for the stock in the problem are based on one sample of observations of the population (population in the context of the time series of a stock's price refers to prices for the stock for all times), we use the central limit theorem to construct a confidence interval for the stock price:

$$\mu - 1.96\sigma < \ln S_T < \mu + 1.96\sigma$$
$$4.0063 - 1.96(0.106) < \ln S_T < 4.0063 + 1.96(0.106).$$

Of course, this confidence interval defines the range in which the natural log of the stock price will fall. We need to calculate the interval for the actual stock price.

Taking the antinatural logarithm of the expression we have

$$e^{(4.0063-1.96\times0.106)} < S_T < e^{(4.0063+1.96\times0.106)}$$
$$2.71828^{3.79854} < S_T < 2.71828^{4.21406}$$
$$\$44.6358 < S_T < \$67.6303$$

Accordingly, one can be 95 percent confident that the stock price will fall somewhere in the interval between $44.6358 and $67.6303 within the next 6 months.

The Use of Trading Days and Calendar Days in Volatility Estimation

Studies have shown that volatility of stock prices is much higher stock exchanges are open for trading compared to the time they are closed.[6] This has led to the practice of considering only the trading days rather than the calendar days in the calculation of volatility of asset prices using historical data. Accordingly, the formula for calculation of annual volatility V^a is given below:

$$V^a = V^{td} \times \sqrt{252} \tag{10.14}$$

where V^{td} is the volatility per trading day and 252 is the number of trading days per year for stocks.

Note that the life of an option is measured in trading days as well as in calendar days. Moreover, T for the options is measured as follows:

T = (number of trading days until option maturity)/252.   (10.15)

To illustrate how to estimate volatility of the price of an underlying asset for options using historical data, we use an example.

Example 10.5

The closing data for Citigroup daily stock price for 21 consecutive trading days appear in the table below.

Table 10.1 Calculation of volatility of daily stock prices of Citigroup

Day	Closing price, S_i	$\dfrac{S_i}{S_{i-1}}$	Daily return $u_i = \ln \dfrac{S_i}{S_{i-1}}$	u_i^2
1	33.67	*	*	*
2	34.79	1.03326	0.032723	0.0010708
3	32.07	0.92182	−0.081409	0.0066274
4	29.71	0.92641	−0.076437	0.0058426
5	29.83	1.00404	0.004031	0.0000162
6	29.03	0.97318	−0.027185	0.0007390
7	28.90	0.99552	−0.004488	0.0000201
8	27.40	0.94810	−0.053299	0.0028408
9	27.30	0.99635	−0.003656	0.0000134
10	25.87	0.94762	−0.053803	0.0028948
11	26.65	1.03015	0.029705	0.0008824
12	26.36	0.98912	−0.010941	0.0001197
13	27.41	1.03983	0.039060	0.0015257
14	27.99	1.02116	0.020939	0.0004384
15	28.31	1.01143	0.011368	0.0001292
16	27.77	0.98093	−0.019259	0.0003709
17	25.39	0.91430	−0.089601	0.0080283
18	26.47	1.04254	0.041657	0.0017353
19	26.01	0.98262	−0.017531	0.0003073
20	29.35	1.12841	0.120811	0.0145953
21	31.60	1.07666	0.073865	0.0054560
			$\Sigma u_i = -0.0634501$	$\Sigma u_i^2 = 0.0536538$

a. Estimate the standard deviation of the daily return.

b. Estimate the annual volatility of the stock price.

c. Estimate the daily volatility of the stock price.

a. The standard deviation of the daily return is

$$s = \left[\frac{0.0536538}{20} - \frac{0.004026}{420} \right]^{0.5} = 0.0517$$

b. Assuming the existence of 252 trading days per year, the annual volatility of the stock is calculated as follows: $(0.0517)(\sqrt{252}) = 0.8207$, or slightly greater than 82 percent.

c. The volatility of the stock return in one day is

$$(0.0517)\left(\sqrt{\frac{1}{252}}\right) = 0.0032,$$ or the stock return has 0.32 percent

daily volatility.

How is the standard deviation used in practice? To illustrate the use of the volatility measure, let the stock price be equal to $31.60. Then a one standard deviation move in the stock price in one day is $31.6 \times 0.0032 = \$0.00512$. As an example, we can cite application of standard deviation as a measure of risk in value at risk analysis.

How Is the Option Value Used in M&A Decision Making?

After valuing the call or put options, the net present value (NPV) is calculated using the following formula:

$$\text{Total NPV} = \text{present value} - \text{investment} + \text{option value}.$$

Example 10.6

A company plans to invest in a project, and seeks to analyze the returns if it postpones investment for 2 years. The data for the investment projects appear below. Using the NPV and real option methods, calculate the investment outcomes.

Investment in year 2 = $50 million
Present value of incremental cash flows = $40 million
Cost of capital = 10 percent
Risk-free rate = r_F= 3.7 percent
Time to maturity = T = 2 years
Strike price = X = $50
Standard deviation = s = 0.15

The NPV Method

$$NPV = 40 - \frac{50}{(1.1)^2} = 40 - 41.322 = -1.322 \text{ million}$$

Real Option Method

Using Formulas 10.4 and 10.5, we calculate d_1 and d_2 as well as the area under the standard normal distribution function:

$$d_1 = -0.597, N(d_1) = N(-0.597) = 0.27525,$$
$$d_2 = -0.80914, N(d_2) = N(-0.80914) = 0.20922,$$

Then we use Formula 10.2, the formula for the European call option:

$$Xe^{(-r_F)(T)} = (50)(2.71)^{(-0.0375)(2)} = 46.39$$
$$c = (40)(0.27525) - (46.39)(0.20922) = 1.30 \text{ million}$$

Accordingly, the NPV of the investment adjusted for the option value is −0.022 million, while the NPV of the investment is a negative return of $1.322 million.

Estimating risks associated with an acquisition emerging from the volatility of cash flows is a challenging task in practice. However, the variance used in the Black–Scholes model can be estimated in several ways. One way is to calculate the variance of the stock prices of the firms in the target firm's industry. For example, an automobile company may use the average of variance of the stock prices of similar automobile companies. Another approach is estimation of the variance of cash flows of similar prior investments. For example, a petroleum exploration company may consider the variance of the cash flows of prior oil exploration projects. A third way is estimation of a measure of volatility of cash flow by the Monte Carlo simulation method.

In a Monte Calro simulation, many alternative scenarios for the net cash flows are estimated by simulating sales, costs, discount factor, or cost of capital, among other factors. The discussion of Monte Carlo is beyond the scope of this book.

Examples of real option valuation in M&As

In this section, we will use examples depicting scenarios for illustration of how one would use real call and put options in target valuation with the option to expand, to delay, and to abandon.

Valuing an Option to Expand

Mardaka Company is negotiating with Zanaca Company, a biotechnology firm, to acquire Zanaca. Based on NPV calculation of Zanaca cash flows, Mardaka can justify the maximum payment of $100 million for Zanaca. However, Zanaca demands a price of $120 million for concluding a deal. Further due diligence by Mardaka shows that combining the resource and technologies of the two companies would lead to more accelerated growth in Zanaca's cash flows. Retooling Zanaca's manufacturing operations, with an estimated cost of $100 million, the acquiring company anticipates a high rate of growth in sales. The present value of Zanaca's cash flows from retooling is estimated to be $80 million. Given the situation, Mardaka cannot justify paying $120 million to conclude the deal.

Subsequent analysis shows, however, that if Zanaca employs Mardaka's new technology, it would acquire the dominant market share changing the market reality altogether. Mardaka believes that it is unlikely that the competitors would develop Zanaca's technology for another 10 years, a period that allows Mardaka to take full advantage of Zanaka's technology for generating higher sales revenues. It is known that the variance of cash flows for the other firms in the industry is 25 percent. The current government bond yield to maturity is 5 percent. Zanaca's patent on the technology will expire in 10 years, which in essence, gives an option with a 10-year expiration date to Mardaka.

Calculate the value of call option to Mardaka, the option to expand by retooling Zanaca's operations. Should it pay the asking price of $120 million?

Solution

The data of the problem are as follows:

Value of the asset (present value of cash flows from retooling Zanaca's operations) $S = \$80$ million

Exercise price (present value of the cost of retooling Zanaca's operations or investment to create the option) $X = \$100$ million

Variance of cash flows $s^2 = 0.25$

Time to expiration $T = 10$ years

Risk-free interest rate $r_{RF} = 0.05$

Using the Black–Scholes formula for call option, we have

$$c = SN(d_1) - Xe^{-r_F T} N(d_2),$$

where

$$d_1 = \frac{\ln\left(\dfrac{S}{X}\right) + r_F T}{\sigma \sqrt{T}} + \frac{1}{2}\sigma\sqrt{T}$$

$$d_1 = \frac{\ln\left(\dfrac{80}{100}\right) + (0.005)(10)}{\sqrt{0.025}\sqrt{10}} + \frac{1}{2}\left(\sqrt{0.025}\right)\sqrt{10} = 0.9655$$

$$d_2 = d_1 - \sigma\sqrt{T}$$

$$d_2 = 0.9655 - \sqrt{0.25}\sqrt{10} = -0.6156$$

$$C = 80N(0.9655) - 100\frac{1}{2.71828^{(0.05)(10)}} N(-0.6156)$$

$$= (80)(0.8315) - 60.653(0.2709) = \$50.08.$$

The NPV of investment in retooling Zanaca's manufacturing operations plus the value of the call option is calculated as $80 - 100 + 50.08 = \$30.08.$

Therefore Mardaka is justified to pay up to $120 + 30.08 = \$150.08$ million to acquire Zanaca.

Note: In calculating $N(d_1)$ and $N(d_2)$, implement the following steps.

1. Consider d_i, $i = 1,2$, as the Z-value and look up a table of areas under the normal distribution curve. In the previous example, for $Z = 0.9655$, $N(0.9655) = 0.3315$, and for $Z = -0.6156$, $N(-0.6156) = 0.2291$

2. Find the area under the curve for the Z-value.

   The area under the curve to the left of $Z = 0.9655$ is $(0.5 + 0.3315) = 0.8315$.

   The area under the curve to the left of $Z = -0.6156$ is equal 0.2709, that is $(1.0-0.5-0.2291) = 0.2709$.

Valuation of Real Call Option to Delay

In the real option to delay investment, the underlying asset is the exclusive right to acquire the target firm. The current value of the asset is the present value of the cash flows from undertaking the project now (S). The option's exercise price is the initial investment in the project (X). The acquiring firm exercises the call option to delay when it decides to postpone investment in the project. The option to delay expires at the time exclusive right to delay expires. However, the delay in investing has an opportunity cost of not having the cash flows during the delay. The annual opportunity cost of delaying the project is $\frac{1}{T}$, for an option that expires in T years.

The presence of the opportunity cost of delaying the investment requires that the formula for the European call option be adjusted. This adjustment of the formula is similar to the effect of dividend payment of stocks on the call price. It is well-known that on the day payment and size of dividend are announced, the stock price drops by the amount of dividend. As a result, the value of the call option on the stock that is to receive dividend is reduced, while the value of the put option on the same stocks is increased. Accordingly the call option formula with the opportunity cost of delaying the investment changes to

$$c = SN(d_1)e^{-DT} - Xe^{-r_F T}N(d_2), \qquad (10.16)$$

where D is the dividend yield or opportunity cost. Note that corresponding to the change in the formula for the call option to delay, the formulas for d_1 and d_2 change as follows:

$$d_1 = \frac{\ln\left(S_0\big/X\right) + \left(r - D - \sigma^2\big/2\right)T}{\sigma\sqrt{T}}. \qquad (10.17)$$

$$d_2 = d_1 - \sigma\sqrt{T}$$

Example 10.7

Being an active player in the M&A market, Mardaka Company considers the acquisition of Laukoy Company, a pharmaceutical enterprise, which has developed a new Alzheimer-fighting drug. The drug has been approved by the government food and drug regulatory agency. The marketing research indicates that this new drug will face a low demand initially due to the existing drugs for the disease. However, it is anticipated that the demand for the new drug will have exponential growth in several years when new applications are identified. Identification of new applications, however, requires $100 million initial investment in research and development. Mardaka Company can delay the investment until the management of the company becomes more confident in the actual growth for the demand for the drug. Moreover, it is believed that it may take 10 years before the competing firms produce a new drug for the same applications.

It is estimated that if the new growth for the drug does not materialize, the NPV of Laukoy Company will be $80 million. In such a case, Mardaka's acquisition of Laukoy is not sensible. The cash flows from previous drug introduction have a variance of 50 percent of the present value of the cash flows. Simulating alternative growth paths for the cash flows generated from the sales of the new drug shows an expected value of $90 million. The 10 year risk-free interest rate is 10 percent.

In spite of the negative NPV of $10 million associated with acquisition of the target, does the value of the call option to delay the initial investment of $100 million warrant acquisition of Laukoy Company?

Solution

Asset value (present value of the expected cash flows from the new drug) $S = \$90$ million

Exercise price (investment required to fully develop the new drug: strike price) $X = \$100$ million

Variance of cash flows $\sigma^2 = 0.50$

Time to expiration $T = 10$ years

Risk-free interest rate $r_{RF} = 0.10$

Opportunity cost of delaying project $D = \dfrac{1}{10} = 0.10$

$$d_1 = \frac{\ln\left(\dfrac{90}{100}\right) + \left(0.1 - 0.1 + \left(\dfrac{0.5}{2}\right)\right)(10)}{\sqrt{0.5}\left(\sqrt{10}\right)} = 1.07$$

$$d_2 = 1.07 - \sqrt{0.5}\sqrt{10} = -1.166$$

First, calculate the area under the normal curve for $d_1 = 1.07$ and $d_2 = -1.165$

$$N(1.07) = 0.5 + 0.2794 = 0.7794$$

$$N(-1.165) = 0.5 - 0.377 = 0.123$$

$$c = (90)\,N(1.07)(2.7183)^{-(.1)(10)} - (100)(2.7183)^{-(.1)(10)}\,N(-1.165) =$$
$$(90)(0.7794)(0.3678) - (100)(0.3678)(0.123) = 21.27$$

The value of the call option to delay is $21.27 million. Hence the NPV of the acquisition is $(S - X + c) = (90 - 100 + 21.27) = 11.27$ million. Therefore, Mardaka should acquire Laukoy Company.

Real Option to Abandon

Situations where the acquiring enterprise has the option to abandon the target are tantamount to having real put options, which is the right to sell. Under such circumstances, the decision rule to continue or abandon consists of comparing the value of continuing the project to its liquidation or sale value. The project should continue if its value is greater than the revenue generated by its sale; otherwise, the project should be abandoned.

The real options involving the right to abandon require that the opportunity cost of investment for the period starting from the time of investment until the time of abandonment be included in valuation of the option. As a result, the Black–Scholes formula for a put option is modified as follows:

$$p = Xe^{-rF} N(-d_2) - Se^{-DT} N(-d_1),$$

where now the d_1 formula has changed to

$$d_1 = \frac{\ln\left(\frac{S}{X}\right) + \left(r - D + \frac{\sigma^2}{2}\right)T}{\sigma \sqrt{T}} \quad \text{and } d_2 = d_1 - \sigma \sqrt{T}.$$

To illustrate how the put options in M&As work, let us use an example.

Example

Exploratory work by the National Petroleum Exploration Company (NPEC) has identified a large petroleum reserve in an oil producing country. To fully develop the resource, NPEC requires $500 million dollars, which is beyond the available financial resource of the company. Global Resources International (GRI) is interested in investing in NPEC; however, the preliminary estimate of cash flow from the extraction of petroleum indicates an NPV of only $500 million (S = $500 million). To attract GRI to invest in the extraction project, the NPEC has offered a $250 million real put option (X = $250 million) to GRI, giving the latter the right to sell its shares to NPEC any time on or before the expiration date of the put option, which is 5 years[7] T = 5). The put option limits the downside risk to NPEC. The variance of the present value of future cash flows is estimated to be 20 percent (σ^2 = 0.2). Since the value of the reserve will diminish over time because of the extraction of petroleum, the present value of the investment will diminish as fewer numbers of cash flows remain with the passage of time. Therefore, one should include the opportunity cost of the right to abandon the project. We assume the opportunity cost as $\frac{1}{n}$, where n is the number of remaining years of profitable reserves. Let the risk-free interest rate be 5 percent. Is the value of the put option high enough to justify investment in the petroleum extraction project?

Solution

Present value of GRI's investment in NPEC $S = \$500$ million

Exercise price of put option $X = \$250$ million

Time to expiration of put option $T = 5$ years

Variance $\sigma^2 = 0.2$

Opportunity cost $\dfrac{1}{T} = \dfrac{1}{5} = 0.2$

Risk-free interest rate $r = 0.05$.

Using the modified formula for the put option, we have

$$d_1 = \frac{\ln\left(\dfrac{500}{250}\right) + \left(0.05 - 0.2 + \dfrac{0.2}{2}\right)5}{\sqrt{0.2}\sqrt{5}} = 0.64314$$

$$d_2 = 0.64314 - 1 = -0.3568$$

$$N(0.64314) = 0.5 + 0.2389 = 0.7389$$
$$N(-0.3568) = 0.5 - 0.1368 = 0.3632$$

$$p = (250)\left(\frac{1}{2.7183^{(0.05)(5)}}\right)(0.7389) - (500)\left(\frac{1}{2.7183^{(0.2)(5)}}\right)(0.3632)$$
$$= 143.86 - 67.66 = 76.20$$

The NPV $(S - X + p) = (500 - 250 + 76.20) = 326.20$ million justifies the investment. Note that the value of the put option is the additional value created by reducing the risk of the undertaking.

Valuation Challenges

The preceding discussions about the methods of valuation of target enterprises are analytical and as such abstract from the complexity of reality.

However, valuation of firms involves a number of practical complications, which the members of the acquisition team should recognize. We discuss these valuation challenges, which appear in all countries, particularly in the emerging economies.

These challenges include:

- Assessing regulatory and market risks
  Assessing regulatory and market risk is a challenging task because prediction of the changing macroeconomic and policy environments is difficult and in many situations impossible. For example, we refer the reader to the regulatory obstacles CITIC, a Chinese company, faced in Australia after the initial capital investment, which is discussed in Chapter 5.
- Unreliable historical financial data
  In many cases, the required data for valuation analysis may not be available. However, in cases when data do exist, their reliability might be questionable, especially in M&As in the emerging economies.
- Collection of debts
  The uncertainty associated with collection of debt could pose additional problems. This is particularly true in many emerging economies, where the contract laws are not well-developed or the legal system is not inclined to enforce the contract laws in a timely manner.
- Questionable capitalization of expenses
  In some instances, the target company might have considered day-to-day expenses, such as expenses related to copying machines, as capital investment. Such false capitalization would distort value of the target and must be identified.
- Inadequate accounting of inventories and receivables
  Inventories and accounts receivable constitute a major part of a company's asset. Therefore detail accounting of these items is important for accurate valuation of the target firm. Moreover, the accounting methods for valuation of inventories are not universal and vary based on the accounting systems used by different countries.

The accounts receivable should be analyzed in determining the creditworthiness of the target company's customers.

- Hidden costs, particularly the cost of labor fringe benefits
  Hidden costs such as fringe benefits for the employees could distort valuation of the target firm. Accordingly, detailed due diligence of hidden costs must be performed before conclusion of an agreement.

- Unreasonable assumptions about financial projections
  Cash flows are the cornerstone of the valuation of an enterprise. Unreasonable assumptions in projection of future cash flows would result in overvaluation of the target company.

- Inadequate financial modeling training of financial model developers
  Financial modeling requires skilled analysts. Analysts with inadequate training and knowledge about financial modeling may provide erroneous financial models and results.

- Unproductive investments in assets such as investment in noncore businesses
  Inadequate attention in determining whether every asset of the target is essential for the core business would result in overvaluation of the target firm. The acquiring company should structure a deal so that only the relevant assets of the target for its core business are acquired.

- Significant contingent liabilities such as tax-related issues and guarantees to third parties
  A contingent liability refers to a liability that may arise upon occurrence of a certain event. For example, a company faces a contingent liability if the product it markets may cause harm to the consumers of the product. The acquiring company should require the target to disclose any potential liability, pending lawsuits, exposure to potential claims, breach of contracts it may have committed, and all claims and liabilities that may not have been disclosed in the financial statements of the target company.

- Valuation of intangible assets

  Intangible assets are important determinants of the profit-ability of a company and should be considered in valuation of the target firm. Intangible assets appear in a variety of forms including marketing-related (trademarks, brand names, service marks, logos, and agreements with the competitors not to compete); customer-related (customer contracts and relationships, customer lists, databases, open purchase orders, distributors, and sales routes); contract-based: (franchise and licensing agreements, permits and contracts, and supplier contracts); technology-based (process and product innovation patents, and related technical documentation, patent applications, proprietary processes and technology, computer software, and copyrights); and artistic-related (musical composition, literary composition, and film copyrights).

  Valuation of intangible assets is a demanding task and should be done by professionals who specialize in this field. We refer the interested reader to ACCUVAL Corporate Valuation and Advisory Services (2013).

- Financial derivatives and instruments

  Increasing use of financial instruments, such as financial derivatives, by companies for management of assets and liabilities in recent years requires critical examination of these instruments by the acquisition team.

Summary

This chapter dealt with a number of important topics including valuation of financial call and put options using Black–Scholes formulas, estimating volatility of returns on the underlying asset from historical data, and use of real options in valuation of target under alternative scenarios of options to expand, to delay, and to abandon. Moreover, challenges in company valuation in cross-border M&As were discussed. Finally, using examples, the differences in company valuation with and without real options were illustrated.

CHAPTER 11

Target Valuation in Cross-Border Mergers and Acquisitions

So far we have discussed target company valuation methods within a country with value expressed in local currency units. However, cross-border mergers and acquisitions (M&As) involve foreign currencies and exchange rates. In this chapter, we will discuss exchange rates, cross-border valuation of cash flows, cross-border valuation of target companies, exchange rate determination, and related concepts and theories.

The Nominal Exchange Rate and Currency Transactions

A nominal exchange rate is the price of one currency in terms of another one. Foreign exchange or foreign currency transactions take place in foreign exchange markets. The foreign exchange market is an over-the-counter market, implying that there is no single physical location, such as the New York Stock Exchange, where traders meet to conduct business. The over-the-counter markets operate by means of electronic communication networks that link the participants, that is, the buyers and sellers of currencies. An overwhelming majority of foreign exchange transactions consist of the electronic transfer of funds from one account into another.

The Exchange Rate Quotation

In the previous section, we defined a foreign exchange rate as the rate at which one currency is exchanged for another one. Accordingly, foreign exchange rates in various countries are defined in terms of the currency of the countries, just as the prices of different products are expressed in terms of monetary units of nations. In China, for example, the prices of commodities, services, and foreign currencies, with the latter as a special class of commodities, are set in Renminbi (RMB). Hence, an automobile may be priced at RMB200,000.00, a shirt may be worth RMB100, or a U.S. dollar is priced RMB6.25. When we price a foreign currency in terms of yuan, such as *RMB6.25 = USD1*, the quotation is given in Chinese term. If we quote the exchange rate between dollar and yuan such as *USD0.16 = RMB1*, we are quoting the currency in *American term,* that is, we are stating the dollar price of one unit of RMB.

When each unit of a foreign currency is quoted in terms of domestic currency, such as *USD0.16 = RMB1*, it is a *direct quotation.* When *each unit* of the domestic currency is expressed in terms of a foreign currency, that is, *RMB6.25 = USD1*, then it is an i*ndirect quotation.*

Indirect quotations are reciprocals of direct quotations. For an example of the yuan–dollar rate, we have

$$RMB6.25 = USD1 \Rightarrow \frac{6.25}{6.25} = \frac{1}{625} \Rightarrow RMB1 = USD0.16.$$

The currency exchange rates are quoted to four decimal places. The fourth decimal (0.001) is called a *point.* If a finer quotation is required, then the currency is quoted to the fifth decimal place (0.00001). The fifth decimal point is called *pip.*

Real Exchange Rate

The definition of exchange rate provided thus far is nominal rate: It does not consider prices in the countries involved. The exchange rate that considers price levels is called the real exchange rate. Real exchange rate compares the value of the home country's goods with the value of the same set of goods of another country. Stating it differently, it is the home currency's purchasing power of foreign goods at the prevailing nominal exchange rate. The real exchange rate is different than the nominal exchange rate, with the latter being the home country's nominal prices of foreign money. The real exchange rate for a currency, Q_t, is calculated by the following formula:

$$Q_t = \frac{S_t P_t^*}{P_t}, \tag{11.1}$$

where S_t is the number of home or domestic currency for a unit of foreign currency at time t, P_t^* is the foreign price index at time t, and P_t is the domestic price index at time t. Note that Q_t expresses price of the domestic goods in terms of foreign goods. For example, we might say a basket of goods in Madison, Wisconsin is worth 250 yuans. Moreover, when one multiplies the nominal exchange rate, which is expressed as the number of domestic currency per unit of foreign currency, by a term that is expressed in units of foreign currency, the result is in units of domestic currency. Accordingly, the right-hand side of (11.1) implies the ratio of average foreign prices that is expressed in the domestic currency unit and the average price level, which is also based on domestic currency, making the average price levels in both countries directly comparable.

Furthermore, note that, to make such a direct comparison of the price levels in the two countries meaningful, one should take care by including the same items in the construction of both indexes. For example, suppose we want to construct a true real exchange rate for RMB and dollar. Also, for simplicity, suppose we have only two items in our composite: MacDonald Value Meal and DVD. So, we would construct a price index for MacDonald hamburger, fries, soft drink, and DVD in China, and we do the same for these goods in America and then use the spot exchange rate to compute the real RMB–dollar exchange rate.

An example would clarify the concept of real exchange rate. Suppose we have three items in the basket: hamburger, French fries, and a soft drink. Furthermore, let the average price of the items in the basket in Beijing be $RMB24$, and in Madison, Wisconsin be $USD5$. Moreover, let the nominal RMB–dollar rate be $RMB6.25 = USD1$. Then using Formula (11.1) the real dollar–RMB exchange rate is calculated as follows:

$$Q_{\frac{\$}{RMB}} = \frac{\left(\dfrac{1}{6.25}\right)(24)}{5} = 0.768$$

and the real yuan–dollar exchange rate is calculated by:

$$Q_{\frac{RMB}{\$}} = \frac{\left(\dfrac{6.25}{1}\right)(\$5)}{24} = 1.3.$$

How should these numbers be interpreted? According to the first equation, 0.768 U.S. basket is the equivalent of 1 Chinese basket, and according to the second number, 1.30 Chinese basket is equivalent to 1 U.S. basket.

Note that the real exchange rate is a measure of competitiveness of a country. If $Q_t \succ 1$, then foreign prices on average are higher than average domestic prices, making the domestic economy more competitive with respect to the foreign country. On the other hand, if $Q_t \prec 1$, then foreign prices are, on average, less than average domestic prices, making the foreign country more competitive. In the previous example of the basket of hamburger, fries, and soda, the U.S. price is lower than the Chinese price for the goods, giving the United States a competitive edge with respect to China in the supply of these products.

The Law of One Price and Purchasing Power

The law of one price states that in the absence of transportation costs and tariffs or other restrictions on international trade, identical goods sold in different countries must have the same price when the prices are expressed in the same currency. Formally, this law can be expressed as follows:

$$P^i_{RMB} = \left({}^{S_{RMB}} / _{USD} \right) \left(P^i_{USD} \right), \qquad (11.2)$$

where P^i_{RMB} is the yuan price of the ith item, ${}^{S_{RMB}}/_{USD}$ is the number of yuan per dollar, and P^i_{USD} is the dollar price of the i_{th} item.

For example, given $RMB6.25 = \$1$, an item that sells for $20 in the United States should sell for $RMB125$ in China, if the law of one price prevails.

Using the formula for the law of one price we can rewrite the relationship as follows:

$$S\,{}^{RMB}/_{USD} = \frac{P^i_{RMB}}{P^i_{USD}}.$$

This equation says that the RMB–dollar exchange rate is determined by the ratio of the price of the item in China and the price of the item in the United States. Of course, this should not come as a surprise to anyone, since if the law of one price holds, this relationship must be valid. However, empirical verification of the law is a totally different, albeit challenging story.

The theory of *purchasing power parity* (PPP) is directly derived from the law of one price, and states that the exchange rate between two currencies equals the ratio of price levels in the countries. Note that the price level of a country reflects the domestic purchasing power of the currency and is the weighted average of a basket of goods and services. Accordingly, the theory predicts that a fall in the domestic currency's purchasing power (a rise in the inflation rate, which is the same as an increase in the price level) leads to a proportional decline in the value of the currency in the country where price level has increased. Accordingly, domestic inflation and value of the national currency are inversely related: When the domestic price level increases, the number of foreign currency required to obtain the domestic currency decreases, which means foreign currency appreciates and domestic currency depreciates. Note that the percentages of appreciation and depreciation of the currencies differ.

Symbolically, therefore, we can express the *absolute* version of the PPP theory as follows:

$$S_\$^{RMD} = \frac{P^C}{P^{US}}, \tag{11.3}$$

where P^C is the RMB price of a basket of goods and services sold in China, and P^{US} is the dollar price of the same basket of the goods and services that are sold in the United States. For example, assuming we have a basket of identical goods in both United States and China, suppose that the RMB cost of the goods in China is RMB1000 and the cost of the same goods sold in the United States is $250; then PPP predicts that the RMB–dollar exchange rate is *RMB*4 = $1.

Note that the law of one price applies to the price of an individual item, while PPP involves the general price level, which is the weighted average of prices of all items in the basket.

Another formulation of PPP theory, known as *relative* PPP, states that the percentage change in the nominal exchange rate equals the difference between the inflation rates in the two countries. Symbolically, if we take the natural log of the formula for the absolute PPP, we come up with the relative PPP theory, that is:

$$\ln\left(S_\$^{RMB}\right) = \ln\left(P^C\right) - \ln\left(P^{US}\right) \Rightarrow \%\Delta S_\$^{RMB} = \%\Delta P^C - \%\Delta P^{US}, \quad (11.4)$$

where the term on the left-hand side refers to the percentage change in the RMB–dollar rate, $\%\Delta P^c$ is the inflation rate in China, and $\%\Delta P^{US}$ is the inflation rate in the United States.

As an example, suppose the inflation rate in China and the United States is 4 percent and 2 percent, respectively. Then the relative PPP model predicts that the yuan price of dollar will increase by 2 percent, that is, yuan depreciates 2 percent.

Exchange Rate Fluctuations

Exchange rates, especially floating rates tend to fluctuate minute by minute, hourly, and daily. The rate of change in exchange rates is called currency *appreciation* and currency *depreciation*. When more units of a domestic currency are needed to purchase one unit of a foreign currency, the domestic currency is said to have *depreciated*, and the foreign currency has *appreciated*. The latter implies that it takes fewer units of the foreign currency to purchase a unit of domestic currency.

The formula to calculate appreciation and depreciation of a foreign currency is given by:

$$\%\Delta S_t = \frac{S_{t-1} - S_t}{S_{t-1}}(100), \qquad (11.5)$$

where S_t is the nominal (spot) rate in the current period t, and S_{t-1} is the spot rate in the previous period.

Example 11.1

Suppose that S_t and S_{t-1} stand for RMB–dollar rate in the current period and the last period, respectively. Given $S_t = 6.25$ and $S_{t-1} = 6.5$, then $\%\Delta S_t = \frac{(6.5 - 6.25)}{6.5} \times 100 = 3.84$. This implies that RMB has appreciated 3.84 percent with respect to the dollar.

Example 11.2

Calculate the rate of dollar depreciation in the previous Example 11.1.

Note that the rates of appreciation and depreciation are not equal. To calculate the dollar depreciation, we must first express the dollar price of RMB, that is, we must express the exchange rate in American term. To do so, take the inverse of 6.25 and 6.5, that is, $\frac{1}{S_t} = \frac{1}{6.25} = \$0.16$ and $\frac{1}{S_{t-1}} = \frac{1}{6.5} = \$0.1538$. This means that the dollar price of one RMB last period was $0.1538, and the price of one RMB this period is $0.16. Therefore, the rate of depreciation of dollar is $\frac{(0.1538 - 0.16)}{0.1538} \times 100 = -4.03\%$.

Spot, Forward, and Swap Currency Transactions

The preceding discussions that differentiate different concepts of the exchange rate are analytical concepts and have important policy applications; however, currency transactions never take place in terms of real or PPP rates. The actual currency transactions involve trading one currency for another one. Next, we will discuss how currencies are exchanged in reality.

Currency transactions take place in four ways: spot market transactions, forward transactions, futures transactions, and swap transactions. The *spot* transaction of a currency takes place when the deal is settled in two business days. The agreed date of payment is called the *value date*.

The *forward contracts* are private agreements between buyers and sellers relating to the exchange of a specific amount of one currency with another one at a specified exchange rate and a specific value date more than two business days. No money changes hands until the value date. The settlement date of a forward contract could be a few days, a week, several months, or even several years. The futures currency transactions are similar to the forward contracts; however, they are standardized contracts that are traded on an exchange. Futures currency contracts are settled daily by the exchanges. Finally, the currency *swap transaction* involves a related spot and forward transaction, where the forward transaction is to reverse the spot transaction.

Note that currency swap transaction as defined in previous paragraph is analogous to spot–forward transaction, which does not involve payment of interest. There exists another kind of currency swap, which involves interest payments on the outstanding currencies exchanged. The second type of currency swap is defined as "...a contractual agreement to exchange a principle amount of two currencies and, after a prearranged length of time, to give back the original principles. Interest payments in each currency also typically are swapped during the life of the agreement" (Butler 2004, 217). Often currency swaps are long-term agreements, the duration for which forward contracts do not exist. We provide the following example of currency swap.

Example 11.3: Currency Spot Transaction

A U.S.-based multinational company purchases $10 million RMB at the exchange rate of $USD1 = RMB6.25$. This implies that the multinational will deposit $10 million in the bank account of the seller of RMB and the buyer of the dollar will deposit $RMB62,500,000$ in the multinational's bank account within two business days.

Example 11.4: Forward Contract Currency Transaction

On June 1, 2013, the foreign currency transaction desk of a multinational bank enters into a forward contract with German exporters of manufactured goods to sell € 100,000 in exchange for Mexican pesos 1,622,847on September 1, 2013.

Example 11.5: Spot–Forward (Swap) Currency Transaction

The Federal Reserve Bank (Fed) requires 10 billion euros today. It contacts the European Union (EU) Central Bank for a swap transaction. The EU Central Bank agrees with the transaction.

The Fed buys 10 billion euros from the EU Central bank in the spot market, and locks in a specific exchange rate by signing a forward contract to sell 10 billion euros in one year.

Example 11.6: Currency Swap Transaction

We illustrate a currency swap with a fixed–fixed rate interest next.

Suppose Company A, a Chinese state owned enterprise, plans to acquire Company B in the state of Wisconsin, United States for $100 million. Even though it could borrow from a government-owned bank in China and covert the fund to dollars for investment in the United States, it prefers to swap currencies (RMB for dollar) with the Citigroup bank in Shanghai. Company A swaps RMB625,000,000 for $100,000,000 with Citi, that is, it deposits RMB625,000,000 in a Citi branch in Shanghai and Citi deposits $100,000,000 in Company A's account in Chicago for 6 months. The swap agreement calls for 6-month London Interbank Rate (LIBOR) + 1.5 points variable rate on $100,000,000 to be paid by Company A to Citi and a fixed rate of 7 percent on RMB to be paid to Company A by Citi in Shanghai. This swap transaction is shown in the following chart:

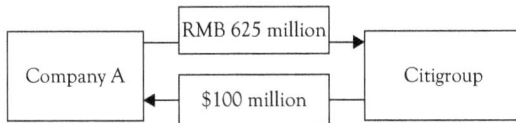

The interest payments for the swap transaction appear in the next flowchart:

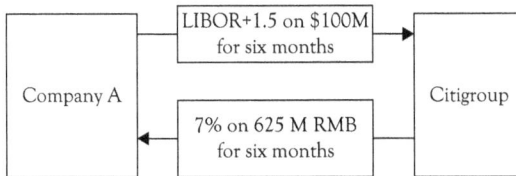

At the end of the swap agreement in 6 months, the swap transaction is reversed by Citigroup paying Company A, RMB625 million in Shanghai and Company A paying Citigroup $100 million in the United States.

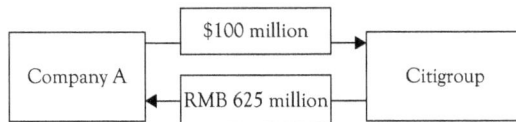

The Relation Between Forward and Spot Rates

The relationship between the spot rate and the forward rate is defined by

$$F = S(1 + p),\tag{11.6}$$

Where F is the forward rate, S is the spot rate, and p is the forward premium.

Example 11.7

The spot dollar–euro rate is $1.56, and euro's 180-day forward premium is 3 percent. Calculate the forward rate.

$$F = 1.56(1 + 0.03) = 1.6068.$$

Example 11.8

The dollar–pound spot and forward rates are $1.56 and $1.75, respectively. Calculate the forward premium.

$$F = S(1 + p)$$
$$F = S + Sp$$
$$p = \frac{F - S}{S} = \frac{1.75 - 1.56}{1.56} = 0.1217$$

Example 11.9

The dollar–pound spot and forward rates are $1.56 and $1.40, respectively. Calculate the discount rate.

$$p = \frac{1.40 - 1.56}{1.56} = -0.1025.$$

Negative premium is called discount rate.

Cross-Border Valuation

In the evaluation of target firms in cross-border M&As, the cash flow denominated in a foreign currency must be converted to the currency of the country of the acquiring enterprise. Therefore, exchange rate plays a prominent role in the valuations. This implies that the discounted value of future cash flows must be converted to the domestic currency units as follows:

$$PV(CF_t) = \frac{\displaystyle\sum_{t=1}^{n} CF_t \times \frac{HC_t}{FX_t}}{\displaystyle\sum_{t=1}^{n}(1+k)^t}, \tag{11.7}$$

where CF_t is free cash flow in *foreign currency* units and $\dfrac{HC_t}{FX_t}$ is the number of *home currency* HC_t per unit of the foreign currency FX_t, at time t, k is the discount rate, and t stands for time.

Example 11.10

Suppose the cash flow from the first year of operation of a target company is $CF_1 = \$1000$. Suppose also that the exchange rate between RMB and U.S. dollar is $USD1 = RMB6.25$. What is the target's cash flow in yuan for the year?

$$CF_1^{RMB} = (\$1000)\left(\frac{RMB6.25}{\$1}\right) = RMB6250.$$

Example 11.11

A China-based multinational enterprise has operations in the United States, which are expected to last 3 years. It is expected that the cost of capital remains unchanged for the duration of the operations. The RMB–dollar exchange rates, the cost of capital, and the expected annual cash flows appear in the following table. Calculate the discounted cash flows in RMB units.

Year	Cash flow in $	Exchange rate	Cost of capital
1	1,000,000	RMB6 = $1	0.1
2	1,500,000	RMB5 = $1	0.1
3	3,000,000	RMB4 = $1	0.1

The ensuing table shows how the present value of discounted cash flows in RMB is calculated.

Year	Discounted cash flow
1	$\dfrac{(1,000,000)(6)}{1+0.1} = RMB5,454,545$
2	$\dfrac{(1,000,000)(5)}{(1+0.1)^2} = RMB6,198,347$
3	$\dfrac{(3,000,000)(4)}{1.331} = RMB9,015,778$
Sum of present values of cash flows in RMB	RMB20,668,670

Note that in this example, because of the depreciating dollar, the value of annual cash flows in RMB would have been higher if the dollar was not depreciating.

Cash Flow Calculation in Multinational Operations in Multiple Currencies

The generalization of the prior discussion in converting cash flows denominated in a foreign currency to cash flows in multiple currencies is straightforward. To calculate the present value of discounted cash flows in multiple currencies, we use the following formula:

$$PV(CF_t) = \sum_{t=1}^{n} \left(\frac{\sum_{j=1}^{m} CF_{j,t} \times \dfrac{HC_{j,t}}{FX_{j,t}}}{\sum_{j=1}^{m}(1+k)^t} \right). \tag{11.8}$$

Example 11.12

A U.S.-based multinational corporation (MNC) has operations in three countries, which are expected to last 3 years. It is expected that the discount rate remains unchanged during the next 3 years. The values of the parameters and the excepted annual cash flows relating to operations appear in the following table. Calculate the value of the MNC's cash flows in U.S. dollars.

Year	China			European Union			United Kingdom		
	Cash flow in RMB	Exchange rate	Cost of capital k	Cash flow in euros	Exchange rate	k	Cash flow in pounds	Exchange rate	k
1	1,000,000	7 RMB/$	0.1	20,000	0.65/$	0.1	10,000	0.51/$	0.1
2	1,500,000	6 RMB/$	0.1	250,000	0.60/$	0.1	150,000	0.60/$	0.1
3	2,000,000	5 RMB/$	0.1	300,000	0.50/$	0.1	200,000	0.65/$	0.1

Solution

Year	China	European Union	United Kingdom
1	$\dfrac{\frac{(1,000,000)}{7}}{(1+0.1)}$	$\dfrac{\frac{(2,00,000)}{0.65}}{1+0.1}$	$\dfrac{\frac{(100,000)}{0.51}}{(1+0.1)}$
2	$\dfrac{\frac{(1,500,000)}{6}}{(1+0.1)^2}$	$\dfrac{\frac{(2,50,000)}{0.60}}{(1+0.1)^2}$	$\dfrac{\frac{(1,50,000)}{0.6}}{(1+0.1)^2}$
3	$\dfrac{\frac{(2,000,000)}{5}}{(1+0.1)^3}$	$\dfrac{\frac{(3,000,000)}{0.5}}{(1+0.1)^3}$	$\dfrac{\frac{(2,000,000)}{0.65}}{(1+0.1)^3}$
Sum	USD637,007.61.	USD1,074,861.76	USD619,603.53
Valuation: USD2.331,472.9			

The last two examples demonstrate the effect of exchange rate variation on cash flows of a multinational enterprise. This is called exchange rate risk exposure. In the next section, we discuss different types of exchange rate exposure and review some remedies to mitigate such risks.

Foreign Exchange Risk Exposure and Mitigation

Foreign exchange or currency risk refers to the impact of exchange rate fluctuations on the performance of an enterprise. There are three kinds of exchange rate risk exposure: transaction exposure, economic exposure, and translation exposure. We discuss these risks in turn.

Transaction Exposure

Transaction exposure refers to the impacts of exchange rate fluctuations on a firm's contractual transactions such as accounts payable and accounts receivable.

Economic Exposure

Economic exposure refers to potential changes in future cash flows resulting from unexpected changes in the exchange rate. For example, foreign currency depreciation impacts exports of an exporting company. Foreign currency appreciation affects imports of an importing company. When a foreign currency depreciates with respect to an exporting company's home currency, the foreign buyers must pay a higher sum of the local currency to import from the exporting company. This tends to reduce the demand for exporters' products. On the other hand, if the foreign currency appreciates (home currency depreciates), the exporting firm must pay a higher sum for its imports and it will have a negative impact on its cash flows.

Translation Exposure

Translational companies consolidate their subsidiaries' financial statements for accounting and tax purposes. Subsidiaries in different countries keep their accounting books in local currency. In the process of consolidation, all accounts denominated in foreign currencies must be converted into the currency unit of the parent company. Because of currency fluctuation, these translations of accounts could adversely impact the cash flows.

A number of methods are used in hedging against foreign exchange risk exposure. These methods include entering into currency forward contract, using currency options, using money market, and swap agreement. Detailed discussions of these methods are beyond the scope of this book. We refer the interested reader to Chapters 11 and 12 of Madura (2008).

Summary

This chapter dealt with the valuation of target companies in cross-border M&As. The discussions dealt with nominal and real exchange rates as well as types of currency transactions such as spot, forward (futures), and swap. Moreover, both absolute and relative PPP theorems were discussed. Also, the relationship between forward and spot exchanged rates was examined. Additionally, cross-border valuation formula and cash flow calculation in multinational operations were used in example data. Finally, different exchange rate risk exposures were reviewed.

CHAPTER 12

Negotiations, Deal Structuring, Financing, and Regulatory Considerations

After valuation of the target firm, the acquiring firm must engage in the important task of negotiations. Negotiation involves implementing several important tasks. These tasks include securing approval for merger and acquisition (M&A), due diligence, refining valuation, deal structuring, identifying sources of financing, regulatory considerations, and postacquisition integration planning. Next we will discuss all but the integration task. Due to the importance of postacquisition integration, we will discuss it in the following chapter.

Strategies to Secure Approval and Approaching the Target

Acquisition of a target firm requires approval from the owners, consent of management of the target firm if it is a public company, the shareholders' agreement in a hostile takeover attempt, and approval from government regulatory agencies.

A formal offer to buy the shares of another firm, for cash or stocks, or both, is called a *tender offer*. In a friendly tender offer, the members of the boards of directors of acquiring and target firms enter into formal negotiations. In some instances, if the board of directors of the target firm rejects such an offer, the acquiring firm may persist on its attempt to acquire the target by approaching the stockholders of the target directly. Such an action is called a *hostile tender offer or a hostile takeover*.

A number of questions should be answered by the acquiring firm when it decides to approach a target firm. These questions include, who should make the initial contact with the target, how the contact should be made, what should be the content of message to the target, which person in the target company should be contacted, and how should the acquiring firm react to the target firm's negative response to engage in M&A negotiations. As a general rule, the highest ranking executive at the target company should be contacted via an intermediary.

Early in M&A transactions, writing a confidentiality agreement and letter of intent is a prudent practice.

Due Diligence

An important phase of negotiations in an M&A transaction is conduct of due diligence as soon as the target firm agrees to allow it to begin. Due diligence refers to a set of activities with the aim of making certain that a potential acquirer obtain what it is intended to get and what it is paying for.

By performing due diligence, the acquiring company will learn about the target company's obligations such as debts, pending and potential lawsuits, leases, warranties, long-term customer agreements, employment contracts, distribution agreements, compensation arrangements, among other financial, technological, personnel, and cultural attributes of the target firm.

Refining Valuation of the Target Company

After the start of negotiation, the task of updating the valuation of the target based on new information and data should begin. The acquirer should request the target's financial data for 3 to 5 years. Based on the internal data of the company that are not available otherwise, the acquiring firm should identify nonrecurring revenues, losses, and expenses.

Deal Structuring

Initial deal structuring is the next step after a preliminary agreement is secured from the target management team. A deal structure is an arrangement between the acquiring and the target firm that defines the rights and responsibilities of both parties.

Deal structuring begins with each party stipulating its own initial negotiating position, identifying potential risks, describing methods of mitigating the identified risks, stating the level of tolerance for risk, and articulating the conditions that permit either party to end the negotiations without reaching an agreement.

Deal structuring processes include tasks such as organizing the acquisition vehicle, designing the postclosing organization, specifying the method of payment, defining the legal form of the selling enterprise, and deciding form of acquisition, as well as accounting and tax considerations. We next briefly define the components of deal structuring.

The *acquisition vehicle* is the legal structure created for acquisition of the target. *The postclosing organization* refers to the organizational and legal framework used for management of the combined business after successful conclusion of the deal. The organizational forms of post-merger entity include corporation, division, holding company, joint venture, partnership, limited liability company, and employee stock ownership plan.

The *form of payment* involves cash, stocks, debt, or a combination of three methods. The *form of acquisition* refers to acquisition of stocks or assets of the target firm. *Accounting considerations* involve assessment of postmerger entity's impact on the financial statements of the acquiring and the acquired enterprises. Finally, *tax considerations* refer to determining whether the transaction is taxable or nontaxable.[1]

Financing Plan

In this phase of the negotiation, the acquiring concern must realistically assess the maximum amount it can finance for investment in the target firm. In financing the transaction of acquiring the target firm, the acquiring firm has the option of using cash in hand, borrowing, issuing equity, and having the seller to finance part of the deal.

Borrowing can take several forms including cash-flow lending, long-term financing, and leveraged bank loans.

In cash flow form of financing, the borrowing is short term, usually less than 1 year in maturity, and the borrowing firm uses certain near liquid assets such as inventory and accounts receivable as the collateral for the loan.

Long-term financing involves issuing of bonds, and leveraged loans, which are noninvestment-grade bank loans. These bank loans have adjustable interest rates, which are usually at least equal to the London Interbank Offer Rate (LIBOR) plus 1.5 percent. Finally, seller financing usually involves the seller agreeing to receive a portion of the purchase price at a later date.

Regulatory Considerations

Governments play prominent roles in regulating cross-border foreign direct investment both in M&A and greenfield forms, as well as regulating business conducts to enhance competition and protect consumers. For example, in the United States, Department of Justice and Federal Trade Commission have the responsibility of promoting competition by enforcing antitrust laws of the United States. The Committee on Foreign Investment in the United States (CFIUS) has the responsibility of reviewing M&As of foreign enterprises in the United States, and report to the president of the United States those mergers or acquisitions that are potential threats to the national security of the United States (see Chapter 5 for the case study involving Ralls Corporation and CFIUS). The Security and Exchange Commission of the United States has strict rules and regulations concerning competitive conduct and governance of publicly traded companies.

Of course government regulations of corporate M&A, either domestically or cross-border, are present in many other countries. Accordingly, in-depth due diligence of regulatory environment of the country where merger or acquisition is to take place is pivotally important. A superficial review of the regulatory environment of the host country could result in huge losses after the conclusion of acquisition.

By way of illustration of deal structuring, we discuss a USD7.1 billion acquisition of Smithfield Foods, a U.S. company, by Shuanghui International Holding Ltd, China's largest pork producer, in September 2013 as a case study. The deal is the largest Chinese acquisition in the United States.

Case Study: Shuanghui International Holding Buys Smithfield Foods

In May 2013, Shuanghui International Holding Ltd, a privately owned Chinese company, announced it will acquire Smithfield Foods for

USD7.1 billion. The acquisition of Smithfield Foods places advanced technology in food production and know-how in food safety regulations, which are deemed to be essential in China's ongoing Five Year Development Plan (2011–2015) at the disposal of the acquirer. In a surprisingly short time, the parties were able to reach an agreement in September 2013. On January 21, 2014, Shuanghui International Holding Limited announced that it has changed its corporate name to WH Group Limited.

Shuanghui International Holding was formerly a state-owned enterprise, which was privatized. Currently roughly 50 percent of its stocks are owned by Goldman Sachs, CDH Investments, Singapore's sovereign wealth fund, and New Horizon Capital, a Beijing-based private equity firm (Gong 2013).

In addition to being the largest Chinese acquisition in the United States, the negotiation that led to an acquisition agreement is unique in several other respects by including an offer that was valid for a limited time, containing a "qualified pre-existing bidder" provision, setting up a unique debt financing structure, and by adopting a strategic approach to the CFIUS review process (Hasting 2013).

The time sensitive offer was submitted to Smithfield Foods in May 13, and received a reply from the target in May 24. On the same day, it was learned that the target was in discussions with two other bidders. On the same day, Shuanghui's attorneys delivered a revised merger agreement to Smithfield, which included an ultimatum that if a deal was not reached by 6:00 p.m. Eastern time, Shuanghui will withdraw the offer. The strategy was to avoid a lengthy, costly bidder war.

The second "qualified pre-existing bidder" provision allowed Smithfield to negotiate with the two existing bidders for 30 days only. However, by signing the merger agreement, Smithfield had to give up its right to seek other bidders.

The third unique feature of the negotiation was creating a two-tier financing arrangement. After reaching an agreement for acquisition, Shuanghui's executives who already had a financing plan, worked with the executives of Smithfield Foods to arrange for an alternative financing plan. The basic idea of the dual financing structure was to optimize Smithfield's postacquisition debt structure. Based on the dual financing plan, Shuanghui entered the U.S. capital market to raise $900 million as part of financing the acquisition.

The fourth unique feature of the deal was a low termination fee of $75 million if Smithfield terminated its agreement with Shuanghui within 30 days of signing the merger agreement. The termination fee is substantially lower than the usual $100 million termination fee.

Finally, another unique feature of the agreement was the exclusion of $275 million termination fee to be paid to Smithfield in case of Shuanghui's failure to secure approval from CFIUS for the acquisition, per term of the merger proposal initially submitted by Smithfield Foods.

Summary

This chapter discussed negotiation, deal structuring, financing options, due diligence, and regulatory consideration for M&As. After defining these terminologies, strategies for securing approval from the target company's management, shareholders, and government regulatory agencies responsible for domestic and cross-border M&As were examined. It was pointed out that detailed regulatory due diligence, especially in cross-border M&As is very important and is instrumental in preventing massive losses after completion of the deal. As an illustrative example of negotiation and deal structuring, the chapter presented a case study of Shuanghui International Ltd acquisition of Smithfield Foods in the United States.

CHAPTER 13

Postmerger Integration and Reorganization

Modern large integrated enterprises consist of many functional units and departments that perform highly specialized tasks that are unique to the units or departments. Managing these separate units or departments requires integration, which consists of coordination, control, and conflict resolution (Shirivastava 1986).

Departments must be coordinated to achieve the overall goals of the enterprise. Control and monitoring ensure that departmental activities are complementary and that departments are performing their specified tasks in a timely manner. Finally, conflict resolution is required to deal with conflicts arising between individuals, departments, or conflicts emerging from inconsistent goals assigned to the departments. Of course, the complexity of organizational integration becomes eminently more complex when independent companies are merged.

The term merger and acquisition (M&A) integration refers to combining two or more business entities after the conclusion of an M&A deal so that the new entity can function as a unified business enterprise.

> Integrating actions '…may involve adapting the firms' value-generating activities to realize technical synergies, altering bureaucratic mechanisms of authority and control to ensure internal coherence, and transforming systems of values, beliefs, and practices to create congruent organizational frames of reference. Thus, integration can be defined as the making of changes in the functional activity arrangements, organizational structures and systems, and cultures of combining organizations to facilitate their consolidation into a functioning whole (Pablo 1994, 806).

The level or degree of integration refers to the extent to which functions or departments of the acquired entity should be combined with the units and departments of the acquiring firm. There is no definitive guideline or consensus on what constitutes the optimal level of integration. However, organizational theorists generally agree that the level of integration depends on the characteristics of merger or acquisition. The characteristics of interest consist of the *task, culture,* and *political* attributes of the acquisition (Pablo 1994). We briefly discuss these characteristics in the context of an acquisition next.

The *task* characteristic, consisting of strategic and organizational, refers to the strategic intent of acquisition, which is based on the recognition that capturing the potential synergies could only become possible by combining two firms. Realization of strategic tasks requires sharing of relevant skills and resources between the acquiring and acquired firms as well as leaving the target company's skills and resources that could lead to synergies intact. The policy of preserving the specialized skills and resources of the target firm is called *organizational task.*

Strategic and organizational tasks have important implications for the degree of integration. These tasks depend on the motivation for acquisitions. If the motivation of acquisition is to capture operational synergies, the need for combing the entities is high. On the other hand, if the motive for acquisition is financial, there is little need for extensive integration.

Culture has important influence on coordination and control functions of integration. Culture plays an important role by generating commitment to the newly created organization, increasing organizational stability in uncertain times of transition, and granting a sense of identity to the members of the organization.

The effect of culture on degree of integration hinges upon the degree of cultural diversity of the acquiring firm. If the acquirer is a multicultural entity, implying that the organization tolerates or encourages cultural diversity, then having an acquired company with a different culture should pose no particular challenges, and the acquirer should leave the culture of the target unchanged. On the other hand, if cultural diversity of the acquiring firm is low, then creation of a more uniform culture across the entities is desirable, and for the purpose of control and coordination, more cultural conformity should be achieved through higher integration.

Political conflicts are omnipresent in all organizations; however, these conflicts tend to increase and become more problematic after M&As. Examples of political conflicts after an acquisition consist of the mandate of new units or departments, the acquirer's misunderstanding of target firm's activities, and the target's failure to comprehend and implement the goals of the acquiring entity. Political characteristics of an acquisition determine the extent power is used by the acquiring firm to resolve the conflict and achieve its goals. The control function of postmerger integration becomes very prominent under such conditions.

Of course, using power by the acquirer in resolving the conflict depends on the perceived need to use power by the acquiring firm and its ability to apply power. Moreover, the perceived need to use power hinges upon the degree of compatibility of visions and actions of the target with those of the acquiring firm. Of course, the size differential between the parties to an acquisition also becomes a determining variable. The larger the acquiring firm compared to the target, the more power the acquiring firm can exercise over the target.

Hence, power differential and compatibility of visions between the acquiring and the acquired firms enter as a guidepost on the level of integration in the acquisition. The level of integration should be inversely related to compatibility of acquisition visions: The more comparable the visions, the lower the level of integration, and vice versa.

In general, postmerger integration involves three types of integration: procedural, physical, and managerial–cultural integration. We will give broad discussions of these integration types next; however, we refer the interested reader to Shirivastava (1986) for detailed discussions of this important topic.

Procedural integration refers to combining the operations, management control as well as strategic planning systems and procedures of target and acquiring companies. The aim of such integration is to facilitate communications between the target and acquiring firms.

Physical integration Involves combination of product lines, production technologies, research and development (R&D), plant and equipment, and real estate assets of companies involved in M&A. The aim of this type of integration is to facilitate resource and know-how sharing between the merged firms.

Managerial and sociocultural integration involves selection and transfer of managers, changes in organizational structure, development of a corporate culture that facilitates achieving the goals of the organization, motivating employees, gaining their commitment, and establishing a new corporate leadership. Achievement of these objectives is a prerequisite to a successful merger or acquisition.

The success of an M&A transaction largely depends on effective postmerger integration and reorganization of former entities. Studies dating back to the late 1960s and early 1970s have shown that a large percentage of failures of acquisitions and mergers are due to ineffective postmerger integration and reorganization (Kitching 1967, 1973). Specifically, among other results, Kitching in his study of 1967 found that in a majority of failures, the organization of the firms was disrupted at least once after the completion of the merger transaction (Hunt 1990).

Statistics of failure of M&A are alarming. According to a Deloitte Consulting LLP (2011) study, 50 percent to 80 percent of all M&A deals fail to live up to expectations. The study shows that in 70 percent of deals, synergies are not achieved, and in a small fraction of the deals, about only 23 percent, the companies earn their cost of capital. Moreover, within the first 6 months, productivity drops by 50 percent, and by the end of the first year, 47 percent of the new company's executives have left. All of these problems, which lead to failure to realize the expected synergies appear to be due to poor planning for M&As, supply chain (SC) disruptions, rising operating costs, and decreasing efficiency (Deloitte 2013).

Furthermore, a survey of members of corporate development teams shows that only 41 percent of respondents were satisfied or highly satisfied by transaction integration of deals they had completed (Ernst & Young 2011). Moreover, a survey of roughly 200 chief executive officers and corporate board members from corporations with annual revenue of $500 million or more in the spring of 2013 showed that "cultural fit," which is the same as postmerger integration, is the most pressing concern relating to M&A for a majority of the respondents. When the respondent was asked to identify the most important risk that is associated with the successful outcome of the postmerger integration process, the respondent identified the factors listed in Table 13.1, with the issue of "cultural fit" as the most pressing concern for many respondents.

Table 13.1 Greatest risk factor for successful postmerger integration

Risk factor	Directors	Chief financial officers
Achieving cultural fit	47%	51%
Synergy capture	25%	11%
Workforce transition	5%	4%
Customer retention	20%	32%
Other	3%	3%

Source: Wall Street Journal (2013).

Approaches to Integration[1]

In general, three approaches to postmerger integration exist: status quo integration, complete integration, and hybrid integration.

First, the status quo integration refers to maintaining the existing conditions. The status quo approach requires that minimal integration of the target with the acquiring company take place. The only area of integration should be financial reporting. Second, complete integration refers to complete acquisition and integration of the target. Third, a hybrid approach, requires that the process will only focus on integrating the best employees, processes, products, services, and technology of both the target and the acquiring company. These approaches may be classified as low, medium, and high levels of integration.

Integration is a complex process that involves simultaneous interactions among all units of an organization. Postmerger integration efforts may be classified into six sets of activities consisting of premerger planning, creating an effective communication mechanism, designing a new organization, developing staffing plans, integrating functions and departments, and setting up a new corporate culture. We briefly discuss these activities next and refer the interested reader to the vast literature on the subject, for example, DePamphilis (2012).

Premerger Integration Planning

A premerger integration plan should make it possible to have a refined estimate of the value of the target company and the transition issues in the context of acquisition agreement. Furthermore, the plan should give the acquirer opportunities to request for warranties, and include conditions for closing that would expedite postmerger integration of the combined companies. Additionally, the plan should create a postmerger integration organization to facilitate integration after closing.

A premerger integration plan as well as involvement of an integration management team in the process should be started as soon as possible, perhaps as soon as valuation of the target has begun. The early start would allow the postmerger integration management team to get familiar with due diligence processes and postmerger integration.

An important component of premerger planning is formation of the postmerger integration organization consisting of staff members from both the acquiring and the target company in friendly M&As. The main tasks of the postmerger integration team include development of a schedule specifying what is to be done, when to do them, and who to do the tasks, determining the economic functions of the combined unit, how to combine the functions and departments, develop performance indicators for both business performance and integration plan, implement the key decisions, and establish communication campaign.

Effective Communication Mechanism

Before public announcement of the acquisition, the management integration team and the public relation department of the acquiring company should prepare communication plans to inform the stakeholders of both target and inquiring entities. Of course, the stakeholders consist of the employees, the stockholders, the customers, the suppliers, and the members of the communities in which the companies involved in the deal are located.

Establishing a New Organization

Structuring an organization consists of devising a division of labor, setting up teams for or departments to do the tasks, for example, production, marketing, R&D, and assigning responsibility and authority to the employees. Implementation of these tasks is tantamount to the creation of a bureaucracy, which provides the rules and regulations that give managers control over employees.

The principles of an organization consist of the following:[2]

1. Unity of command
   Only one person should be in charge.
2. Hierarchy of authority
   Workers should know who they should report to.
3. Division of labor
   Functions should be divided into areas of specialization, for example, production, finance, and marketing.
4. Subordination of individual interests to the collective interest
   This implies that workers should consider themselves as a member of the team.
5. Authority
   Authority means that managers have the right to give orders.
6. Degree of centralization
   Degree of centralization refers to vesting of power to top management. The degree of power should depend on the circumstances and size of the organization. All power should be vested in top management of small organizations, and in large enterprises some power should be given to lower level managers.
7. Clear communication channels
   In an organization with clear communication channels, employees at all levels can readily and quickly communicate with each other.
8. Order
   In an organization with a high degree of order, all materials and people are placed and maintained in proper locations.
9. Equity
   Equity implies that all employees should be treated fairly and equitably.
10. Promotion of company spirit
    The pride and loyalty about the organization should be maintained.
11. Job description
    The nature of the jobs should be described in writing.
12. Written guidelines and decision rules
    All guidelines and decision rules should be written down and detailed records should be maintained.

13. Consistent policies

All procedures, regulations, and policies should be consistent and should not contradict each other.

14. Qualifications as the basis for promotions

Staffing and promotions should be based on qualifications of the employees.

In setting up a new organization, the management must consider the following issues:

a. Centralization versus decentralization

In a centralized organization, decisions are made at the top management level at the corporate headquarters, while in a decentralized organization some less sensitive decisions are made by lower level managers.

b. Span of control

Span of control refers to the optimum number of workers under the supervision of a manager. In a business environment where tasks are more or less similar and standardized, for example, jobs in an automobile assembly plant, one could supervise more workers than the situation where tasks are more heterogeneous, for example, a large R&D division with many innovation projects that are being developed simultaneously.

c. Tall versus flat organization structures

Tall organizations are pyramidal structure enterprises that have many layers of management. Flat organizations have fewer layers of management but a broad span of control.

d. Departmentalization

Departmentalization refers to organizing different functions of an organization, functions such as production, marketing, finance, and so forth, into different units. Departmentalization of a business organization can take different forms, including departmentalization by products or services (products X, Y, Z), by functions (production, marketing, and so forth), by customer group (consumers, commercial users, manufacturer, government), by geographic locations (European Union, Middle East, Far East, North America,

Latin America), by process (jet engine, fuselage, landing gears, communication electronics, navigation electronics), and divisional in which families of products are grouped together into independent divisions. The divisional form of organization is commonly used by conglomerate enterprises such as General Electric Company, which has consumer and commercial finance, aviation, health, energy, and transportation divisions.

Organizational Model

Organizations can be designed using three different models: line organization, line-and-staff organization, and matrix organization.

According to the line organization model in two-way lines of responsibility–authority, the communications are conducted from the top to the bottom of the organization, and all employees report to only one supervisor.

In a line-and-staff organization, the employees of a firm are classified into two categories: line personnel and staff personnel. The line personnel are responsible for achieving the goals of the enterprise directly, while the staff personnel advise and assist line personnel in achieving the goals of the enterprise.

Finally, in a matrix-style organization, specialists from different departments are organized into units that work on specific projects; however, these employees remain as part of the line-and-staff organizational structure. In a matrix-style organization, project managers are in charge of the members of the team.

The first important task in creating a new organization is appointment of members of the top management team. The leaders for departments, functions, and groups must be identified and their responsibilities should be clearly defined. Next, the structure of the new organization as previously discussed must be specified.

Developing Staffing Plans

Staffing plan or human resource (HR) management consists of determining HR needs, recruiting, motivating, scheduling, evaluating, and compensating employees to achieve the goals of the organization.

Staffing plan should be undertaken in postmerger integration processes as soon as possible, and key employees from both acquiring and target companies should be included in staff planning for the new entity. The staffing strategy should focus on personnel requirements, employees' availability, needs for external recruitment, compensation, and personnel information system.

Integrating Functions and Departments

Integration of functions and departments involves integration of planning and strategy; finance and administration; human resources; information technology (IT); supply change management; postacquisition business processes and internal controls; intellectual property (IP) rights protection and management. We discuss each of these integration processes next (Deloitte 2013).

Planning and Strategy

As stated earlier, a pivotal factor in a successful M&A transaction is planning and implementation of integration of the target firm with the acquiring firm. The challenge of planning is how to design a new strategy so that the new entity captures the potential benefits of the transaction without having negative impacts on financial performances of target and acquiring companies. A plan for successful transaction embodies three important components: clear statement of the purpose of the transaction, control of the M&A processes so that they do not negatively affect day-to-day operations of the entities, and managing employees.

Finance and Administration

Integrating the financial functions entails reorganizing the financial management and budgeting processes. A successful plan for financial integration must involve consolidating the financial and accounting functions of the entities involved, and capturing the synergies of the transaction, that is, cost reductions. Specifically, designing financial as well as accounting, including tax-related accounting, processes involves changing sales to accounts receivable cycle, purchases to accounts payable cycle, investment to fixed assets cycles, tax compliance process, and book-closing cycle for the new enterprise.

Of course, financial assets (cash, stocks, and bonds) as well as physical assets (equipment, plants, inventories, raw materials and intermediate inputs, real estate) and intangible assets (brand name, copyrights, exclusive agreements, product quality, technological patents, trade secrets, software) of acquiring and target firms should be combined and controlled.

Human Resources Integration

Human resources integration planning is as important as the other aspects of postmerger integration planning for success of an M&A transaction. Integration of HR departments of the target and acquiring companies implies that approaches to recruitment, retention, compensation, training, and other aspects of personnel management of the companies must be unified. A 2005 survey of timing of HR integration indicates that 40 percent of respondents started integration of HR at the time of due diligence, 24 percent began the process at the start of M&A deliberation, and the remaining 36 percent began the process at the time of integration of the acquired company (Reed, Lajoux, and Nesvold 2007).

Typically HR integration involves five categories: organization design, compensation, employee compliance, retention of key employees, and elimination of redundancy.

Organization design should take place soon after the signing of the sales–purchase agreement, and should be completed before the closing date. In designing the organization, consideration of cultural differences of the organization involved should play an important role.

In general, the target company's HR policies converges to with the HR policies and practices of the acquiring company. The staff for the new organization should include key employees from both organizations, and the compensation of the employees of the new business should be commensurate with the compensation of the employees of the acquiring company. In cross-border acquisitions, local employment laws, rules, and regulations should be examined.

Employee compliance with applicable laws, rules and regulations, and company's code of ethics requires wide distribution of the policy statement about these topics. The corporate policies concerning ethics and security should be well-defined for the employees of the new organization.

Key employees from the target company must be identified at an early stage of the M&A processes by having the target to secure an agreement to retain the key personnel for at least 6 months to 1 year.

In any M&A transaction, redundancy of employees inevitably occurs. The reorganization plan of the HR department should provide new opportunities for the redundant staff members to be retained for employment in a different capacity. For those employees whom the problem of redundancy cannot be dealt with, adequate severance payment should be provided based on the prevailing customs, rules, or laws.

Integration of Information and Communication Technology

Large public and private organizations rely on their information and communication systems for timely, reliable, and accurate information that is often crucial for optimal decision making. Accordingly, timely integration of information and communication technology (ICT) is pivotally important in capturing the benefits and synergies of a merger or acquisition. The negative impact of delaying integration of communication and information systems of the target and the acquiring company depends on the strategic level of intended interdependence or autonomy of firms involved in merger or acquisition.

It is useful to have a clear knowledge of the components of ICT for the purpose of integration.

An ICT system consists of the following:

1. Information systems (databases and processing functionalities)
2. IT infrastructure (data networks, operating systems, hardware, IT skills)
3. IT policies (procedures for users and IT managers and IT management, IT coordination, education, and support)
4. Communication device or application, including radio, television, cellular phones, computer and network hardware and software, satellite systems, and so on; videoconferencing; and distance learning

Of course much of communication technology uses computer-enabled devices, hence the term ICT.

In general three *integration strategies* are adopted in M&As. First, the acquirer might choose the strategy of complete *absorption* of the target firm by unification of management systems of the target with the acquirer. Second, the acquiring firm might adopt the *symbiosis* strategy, which implies cross-transfer of selected capabilities and resources of the involved companies, while retaining the identity and autonomy of both firms. The third strategy is preservation strategy, which refers to the strategy of the acquiring company to nurture the capabilities of the target, while maintaining the target's autonomy (Haspeslagh and Jemison 1991).

Clearly, the role of ICT in the first case (the absorption approach) of the target is the most important, and we will discuss factors contributing to the speed of ICT integration, which is an important determinant of the success of M&A.

Strategy for ICT Integration

A strategy for ICT integration aims to establish a desired level of integration of the ICT systems of target and acquiring companies. An ICT strategy contains ICT objectives and methods of achieving them (Wijnhoven et al. 2006).

Corresponding to ICT integration strategies previously enumerated, ICT integration objectives depend on IT integration ambition levels, where the ambition level could be complete integration, partial integration, or marginal integration. Complete integration may be infeasible in cases where large enterprises are involved, while it is doable for smaller firms. Partial integration establishes priorities, and first integrates the most important processes, leaving the less important ones for later. The prioritization is based on synergies the processes could generate. Finally, marginal integration leaves most items intact and implements bridges for data exchange and consolidation when absolutely required (Wijnhoven et al. 2006).

The ICT *integration methods*[3] consist of maintaining the status quo, eliminating the ICT of one company while maintaining and adapting the ICT of the second one, creating a hybrid using both ICT systems, discarding the old ICT systems and adopting a new one, and finally out-sourcing (Harrell and Higgins 2002).

In using the absorption strategy of ICT integration, a number of questions must be answered including (Harrell and Higgins 2002):

- How to structure the information system of the new firm?
- Which company's strategy should be adopted if any?
- What technology should be used for the merged entity?
- What are the cost savings of combining the two ICT systems?
- Where the data centers are to be located and where application software, databases, and hardware are to be kept?

In any event, the merging companies should plan for an ICT system at the due diligence stage and not after securing a deal. At this early stage, the acquiring and target firms should exchange information about their respective ICT infrastructures, hardware, and software.

The task should be performed by small internal transition teams, which are empowered and capable of implementing the task. Assessment of the size, scope, and functionality of the current ICT systems; and information gathering about business processes, the supply chain management (SCM), as well as the size and locations of the files should be carried out.

During the entire postmerger integration process, the goal should be implementation of the infrastructure change with minimal impact on consumers, the employees, and the stock prices of the companies.

Supply Chain Management Integration

A corporate strategy that has a holistic view of operations, materials, and logistics management is called supply chain management.

A variety of definitions for the term supply chain management is used in the literature on the topic. Among the three definitions that appear in Tan (2001), we believe the following definition is the most appropriate one in the context of our discussions of M&As. SCM refers to "… the integration of the various functional areas within an organization to enhance the flow of goods from immediate strategic suppliers through manufacturing and distribution chain to the end user" (Tan 2001, 40).

From this definition, we could infer that the intensity of integration of SCM of target and acquiring entities depends on whether the merger is vertical or horizontal. In a vertical merger or acquisition, the SCM of the entities is already integrated, even though such integration may not be optimal. Any additional integration in such cases must be confined to internal integration of the existing SCM of the organization. Acquisition of a customer or a supplier implies acquisition of an entity that already exists in the SC of the acquiring firm. Hence, discussions of integration of SCM in the context of M&A only pertain to integration of enterprises in a horizontal merger or acquisition. We will discuss integration of SCM in horizontal mergers or acquisitions presently.

A Short History of SCM

The emergence of SC as an important corporate strategy goes back to 1980s, when the competitive global business environment forced many large integrated enterprises to offer low cost, high quality, and reliable products. One of the innovative approaches in achieving this goal was utilization of just-in-time (JIT)[4] and other management initiatives that reduced the cost of holding inventories. However, the JIT system of inventory required formation of business alliances, and buyer–supplier relationships. Moreover, many of the buyers relied and continue to rely on their supplier's technology in development process and product innovations. In fact for companies that use the JIT inventory control system, the IT systems of the customer's procurement department are integrated with the supplier's IT systems to form a seamless procurement mechanism. Attempts to increase the pattern of interdependence between the suppliers and customers lead to the adoption of corporate strategy of SCM, which aims to create seamless manufacturing and logistic functions as the integrated SC strategy. This strategy is a preemptive, competitive weapon to hinder duplication of the SC process by the competitors.

Optimal Supply Chain and Corporate Performance

A well-integrated SC consists of optimal flows of materials, products, and information between suppliers, manufacturers, and customers. Of course, optimal design of such a network relies on system-optimization methods such as linear and nonlinear programming, the discussions of which are beyond the scope of this book. We recommend the interested reader to consult Nagurney (2006) for further discussions of this topic.

Firms with strong integrated global SCM teams are found to cooperate with their suppliers and customers more effectively. These firms tend to innovate, manufacture, store, market, and supply better after-sale services more efficiently with greater speed.

A study conducted by Accenture, with collaborative research efforts of INSEAD[5] and Stanford University used data from more than 600 Global 3,000 companies and found statistically significant relationship between SC performance to increase in stock prices of the companies and rise in shareholder value (Accenture 2003).

Why does a well-integrated SC result in better financial performances of companies? The answer is that an optimally integrated SC creates synergies.[6]

Synergy creation by optimal integration of the SC emerges from the optimal level of inventory (or minimization of working capital), better services, improved distribution network, faster shipment–shorter order-to-cash cycle, and leveraged purchasing processes (Langabeer and Seifert 2003). Of course, creation and capturing such synergies could be a powerful motive by combining enterprises through M&As.

Why does optimal integration of SC matter? Studies have shown that difficulties in successful postmerger integration of SC of the target and acquiring companies are major contributing factors to the failure of the merger. For example, in a 2007 survey by Accenture, which questioned 154 managers, about two-thirds of respondents revealed that they experienced increased disruption in their business operations due to M&As. About 50 percent had problems with supplying orders, and more than 40 percent of the respondents reported experiencing problems in inventory management (Zhu, Boyaci, and Ray 2013).

One of the reasons for the failure of M&As is that SC professionals are not included as members of M&A teams, in spite of the fact that operational costs are the major portion of the total costs of any enterprise. It is common knowledge among executives responsible for M&As that executives who are responsible for planning in many corporate mergers (finance and accounting professionals) are different individuals than those employees who are to implement postmerger integration. The latter executives are SCM professionals. The exclusion of SC professionals in the early phase of M&A negotiation and planning takes place in spite of their greatest interactions with the customers of the acquired company.

The success of SC integration and capturing synergies of M&A deals hinges upon implementation of two policies: inclusion of SC professionals in the early phases of the M&A negotiations and development of integration strategy.

First, inclusion of SC professionals in the earlier stages of M&A negotiation and planning enables them to identify the synergies that could result from the merger or acquisition. Second, M&As provide opportunities for corporate executives to reconstruct the company's business model and develop new operations perspective and strategies by raising key strategic what-questions: what markets, what products, and what locations? Formulating interim-state and end-state SC visions and degree of integration of SC hinges upon answering these what-questions (Shirivastava 1986; Deloitte 2013).

Second, inclusion of SC professionals as members of the acquisition team enables the executives to concentrate on formulation of business strategy for the combined companies, while the SC professionals work on developing operations plan for the new entity. Under such conditions, the likelihood of capturing synergies from the acquisition increases.

Formulation of integration strategies depends on the relative size of the target firm with respect to the size of the acquiring firm as well as on the desired degree of integration. The operations integration of an acquiring firm with a target that has only, for example, 5 percent of its revenue would be dramatically different if the target's revenue were higher than the revenues of the acquirer (Larsson and Finkelstein 1999).

Based on the scale of acquisition, four kinds of integration plans for SC exist. These integration strategies fall into four categories: *transformation, bolt-on, consolidation, and tuck-in.*

A *transformative* integration strategy requires a new organization structure that affects the existing processes and value chain of previously independent organizations. A *bolt-on* strategy means the target is acquired but is operated as a portfolio enterprise and has independent processes and structure. *Consolidation* strategy involves large acquisitions and requires additional resources for SC integration. Finally, in the *tuck-in* strategy key assets of the target are absorbed into the acquirer's current operation with little or no integration (Deloitte 2013).

It has been found that large size differential between acquiring and acquired firms does not help success (Hunt 1990). Of course, the effect of level of integration between the bidder and target firms on the performance outcome of the combined firm is indeterminate. Studies have shown both positive and negative impact of the degree of integration on performance of the combined firm (Zarb and Noth 2012). Therefore, no general statement and policy recommendation concerning the extent of integration can be suggested. One should consider the specifics of an M&A deal to determine the optimal level of integration.

Degree of Integration

The level or degree of integration is the extent of postacquisition change in the organizational, technical, administrative, and cultural setups. Defining the correct degree of integration is important because a high level of integration under all circumstances does not necessarily lead to efficient outcomes, and could be a source of negative synergies resulting from high coordination costs and increasing the likelihood of interorganizational conflict (Pablo 1994).

Motives for Acquisition and Supply Chain Integration

In planning for SC integration, the motive for the acquisition must be specified in terms of synergies it might generate. What are the sources of synergies? Are synergies emerging from production, marketing, R&D, and administration, or do they come from an increase in market power as a seller or buyer? Do the synergies originate in the replacement of incompetent executives by competent ones, or are synergies created by financial and other risk diversifications? What competitive advantage does the acquisition provide? What types of SC disruptions would take place after closing? What is the appropriate level of SC integration? Studies show that these questions are seldom raised before closing (Tyndall 2010).

Actions for Rapid Supply Chain Integration

In any event, studies have found that the speed of SC integration is an important determinant of the success of the merger or acquisition. Companies that did not have much success in capturing the synergies they thought they would gain from acquisition required at least 2 years in integrating the SCM systems of the target and acquiring companies. The successful firms, in contrast, completed integration of SCM within the year of completion of the deal (Langabeer and Seifert 2003).

Planning for SC integration should begin during the initial month of M&A due diligence and negotiation. A list of policies for an effective, rapid postmerger integration of SCM of the companies in mergers or acquisitions appears as follows (Langabeer and Seifert 2003).

1. Be sensitive to customers' needs and concentrate on execution.
   Losing customers because of customers' dissatisfaction and inadequate handling of orders is an irreversible process. Lost customers are hard if not impossible to gain.
2. Identify the important SC organizations and their leaders.
   Decision-making processes and management control should be well-defined for the merged SC. The executives and managers for integration of SC of the new entity must be identified in the early stages of M&A negotiation processes.
3. Do not assume the current business model is optimal.
   The dominant company should not assume its current business model is optimal. Assess strategy, systems, staff members, processes, and networks.
4. Develop performance indicators and clear execution channels.
   M&As create a great deal of uncertainty for the current employees of the companies involved. The uncertainty often results in less than optimal performance by the employees. Having performance indicators and making sure the tasks are effectively being executed could minimize distractions.
5. Develop and monitor an integration time line.
   Deadlines should be established and employees are to be held accountable for meeting the deadlines.

Adopting these policies in integrating SC could assist, if not guarantee, capturing four types of synergies resulting from M&A (Herd, Saksena, and Steger 2005).

Revenue

A well-designed SC ensures customers' satisfaction by filling the orders without interruption, hence avoiding loss of revenue during times of transition.

Operating Expense

Supply chain is an important determinant of the cost of production of goods and services, and degree of effectiveness of supply line has a direct impact on operating expenses as well as the net income of the enterprise.

Capital Expenditure

The outlays on physical assets involved in SC, assets such as manufacturing plants, warehouses, telecommunication, IT, and transportation equipment, are very large. Optimal SC sourcing and operations have a major positive impact on company's cash flows by minimizing investment in these assets.

Working Capital

How quickly and efficiently a firm can convert raw materials into finished goods and have them available for consumers' use can strongly affect the company's cash flow.

Forming a New Corporate Culture

Commonly three sets of problems emerge during the integration phase of M&As: cultural (organizational and national) conflicts, selecting a new management team, and encouraging employees to welcome the employees of the target firm. We discussed corporate culture in Chapter 4 and used the following definition for it: "the part of the stock of knowledge that is shared by a substantial portion of the employees of the firm, but not by the general population from which they are drawn" (Cremer 1993, 354). Here we discuss some policies in remedying the cultural integration problems of cross-country M&As, which are based on a survey of a sample of top management (chief executive officers, chief financial officers, vice presidents of business development) of active acquiring firms in France, Germany, Italy, and the United States (Very and Schweiger 2001). These measures include:

1. Offering of intercultural management workshops that help employees to get familiar with each other
2. Building mutual trust by frequent visits of operational managers of acquiring and target firms
3. Informing the target employees about the benefits of being employed by the acquirer by top management of the acquiring firm
4. Transferring of acquiring firm's managers to manage the acquired one
5. Seeking help from local consulting firms on cultural integration
6. Retaining top management of the acquired firm after the completion of the deal
7. Adjusting organizational structure of the acquiring firm to facilitate integration of the target

Postacquisition Processes and Internal Controls Integration

The main objective in postacquisition integration of operations is reduction of the average costs of production, inventory, marketing, and distribution by integrating similar departments and functions. However, in practice, incompatibility of variables such as management styles, systems of evaluation of compensation, and organizational cultures are major impediments in achieving the objective (Datta 1991).

We have discussed organizational culture and related issues in previous chapters, particularly in Chapter 4. However, we briefly review the remaining concepts of management style and evaluation–compensation system that determine organizational fit here.

Management style refers to the management's attitude toward risk, the method of management decision making, and their preferred approach to control and communication (Datta 1991; Covin and Slevin 1988). Clearly, management styles across business organizations tend to vary considerably, and when two incongruous management styles from the combining firms come together in managing the new entity, a major conflict in the control of the new organization could arise.

Evaluation and compensation systems vary considerably across organizations and industries. Studies have shown significant differences among evaluation criteria companies use for evaluating managerial performance (Lorsch and Allen 1973; Bloom and Van Reenen 2006). Accordingly, when management teams come together from different reward and evaluation systems in the new company, the potential for conflict increases. The new management team should establish levels of authority, integrate business processes and internal controls, and establish and implement monitoring controls.

Postacquisition IP Rights Management and Control

Intellectual property (IP) is an important asset that is transferred in M&As. By the transfer of IPs, the merged entity could discover overlapping or complementary IP assets. In certain M&A situations, the acquiring and target companies may have combined IP rights that would form a formidable barrier to entry into the industry; hence this may create a privileged monopoly situation for the new firm. Accordingly, the issues of patents, IP rights, and the adverse effects of M&As on consumer welfare by constraining innovations are surely to arise in M&As. These are important issues that must be addressed in premerger due diligence and postmerger integration. This is an important topic, but it is beyond the scope of this book. We refer the reader who is interested in the details of this topic to Durand (2005).

Nevertheless, the essential task at the postmerger integration stage is determination of combined IPs of the merged companies. The IP assets should be categorized as fully protected and not protected. Of course, some of the IP holdings would fall in between these two extreme cases for being somewhat protected. Having prepared a list of IPs owned by the new entity, the next task is learning what each IP does, and what the new entity wishes to achieve. After implementing these two tasks, the postmerger implementation team should develop an IP strategy for the new company (Tayler Vinters Solicitors 2010).

Postmerger Acquisition Practices in Asia

A recent study by Cogman and Tan (2010) indicates that the required fast-paced postmerger integration, model, which is based on practices of executives of Western companies, has not been followed by executives in many recent acquisitions in Asia. The authors wrote:

> In a recent review, we estimated that roughly half of all Asian deals deviated significantly from the traditional postmerger integration management model, which aims for rapid integration and the maximum capture of synergies. Over a third of the Asian deals involved only limited functional integration and focused instead on the capture of synergies in areas such as procurement, with an overwhelming emphasis on business stability. An additional 10 percent attempted no functional integration whatsoever (Cogman and Tan 2010, 8).

The reason the authors give for such practices is difference in attitudes of Asian and Western executives toward risk. The Asian executives are accustomed to organic internal growth rather than growth through M&A; many Asian executives aim to minimize the short-term risk of failure. Their aim is long term. They tend to trade capturing the immediate benefits of synergies for gaining the long-term benefits of expanding into new and unfamiliar markets, introducing new product lines, and gaining technological and marketing capabilities. Moreover, the managements of the acquiring companies by not making fundamental changes in the managements of the acquired entities give themselves opportunities to learn operational details of the target firms.

With this background discussion about postmerger integration, we present the following case study relating to possible issues that could arise in both domestic and cross-border M&As. Another case study pertaining to postmerger integration practices of a Chinese company is presented in Chapter 15.

Case Study: Labor Conflict in Postmerger Integration

On November 29, 2013, *China Daily* reported that many workers of the Nokia factory in the southern Chinese city of Dongguan went back to work after they went on strike against the company on November 19, 2013. The workers were concerned about a possible wage and benefit cut due to a merger between the Finnish telecom company Nokia, and U.S. giant Microsoft Corporation.

The strike began on the same day Nokia announced that its shareholders had approved the $7.2 billion acquisition deal according to which Nokia would be acquired by Microsoft in early 2014.

Established in 1995, Nokia's plant in Dongguan employs roughly 32,000 workers with 4,900 staff members producing mobile devices for the company.

The striking workers demanded a new contract with equal or better compensation terms for workers to be signed by Microsoft, before closing the merger deal.

The workers ended the industrial actions after Microsoft agreed that the workers' salaries and benefits would remain unchanged for 12 months after completion of the acquisition.

China Daily also reported that the managers of Dongguan factory rewarded nonstriking workers 1,000 yuan or $164 for not taking part in the strike, and terminated the employment of those who did strike. In fact, at the time of reporting more than 200 striking workers were terminated.

Moreover, similar types of Chinese worker strikes concerning cross-border M&As in China have occurred. These strikes involved cross-border deals such as Western Digital's purchase of Hitachi Global Storage Technologies and Indian tire maker Apollo's attempted acquisition of Cooper Tire & Rubber, a U.S. Company (Xinhua, 2013).

Summary

This chapter deals with postmerger integration. It was stated that the failure of most M&As to realize the synergies that were envisioned before the acquisition is a result of difficulties of integrating the acquired and acquiring companies. After a brief review of approaches to postmerger integration, it was stated that integration plans should be devised in the early stages of M&A activities. Furthermore, different aspects of integration including integration of functions and departments were reviewed. Finally, some policies for organizational as well as national cultural integration were suggested. A case study was presented by way of illustration of difficulties companies could face in postmerger integration processes.

PART II

Cross-Border M&A Activities of Chinese Enterprises

Given the increasing importance of China as the second largest economy in the world and Chinese companies' growing merger and acquisition (M&A) activities both inside China and globally, we devote the next part of the book to China's outward foreign direct investment and cross-border M&A activities.

CHAPTER 14

China's Outbound Foreign Direct Investment

This chapter deals with the development of China's outbound foreign direct investment (OFDI) activities over the last three decades. In addition to discussions relating to size and geographic distribution of China's OFDI, we review the motives for Chinese companies to acquire companies abroad. Furthermore, China's rules and regulations for outbound mergers and acquisitions (M&As) are discussed.

China has been playing an increasingly important role not only in international trade but also in international capital flows both in portfolio and foreign direct investment (FDI) forms since the 1990s. In this book, we only focus on OFDI by Chinese enterprises, even though portfolio and direct capital flows to and from China are significant. However, discussions of these topics are outside the scope of the present book.

At the start of 2011, more than 13,000 Chinese entities had established roughly 16,000 overseas enterprises in 178 countries (regions) (Ministry of Commerce 2013). The status of China as the sixth-largest international investor in 2011, changed to the third largest ($84 billion) in 2012 (Sauvant and Chen 2013).

Table 14.1 shows the global distribution of the outward foreign direct investment flows for China from 2004 to 2010.

To gain a better appreciation of the geographic distribution of China's overseas direct investments (ODI) by countries, we refer the reader to Table 14.2. The table shows the top five recipients of Chinese direct investment by continents. Note that for North America and Oceania, China invested only in three countries in each, and have only three countries listed for the continents.

Table 14.1 *Global distribution of China's outbound foreign direct investment flows (USD million): 2004–2010*

Region	2004	2005	2006	2007	2008	2009	2010
Asia	3013.99	4484.17	7663.25	16593.15	43547.5	40407.59	44890.46
Latin America	1762.72	6466.16	8468.74	4902.41	3677.25	7327.9	10538.27
Europe	2046.77	2166.65	597.71	1540.43	875.79	3352.72	6760.19
North America	126.49	320.84	258.05	1125.71	364.21	1521.93	2621.44
Africa	317.43	391.68	519.86	1574.31	5490.55	1438.87	2111.99
Oceania	120.15	202.83	126.36	770.08	1951.87	2479.98	1888.96

Source: Ministry of Commerce, People's Republic of China (2013).

We make several comments with respect to the investments in Table 14.2. First, the capital outflow from China to Hong Kong was $38505.21 million in 2010, which is the largest sum of capital flow in Asia. However, Hong Kong is a Special Administrative Region of the People's Republic of China, and we do not consider capital flows from China to this region, foreign capital flows. Second, the large investment in Sweden in 2010 is an aberration of China's investment in that country and is due to acquisition of Volvo by the Chinese carmaker Zhejiang Geely Holding Group from Ford Motor Corporation. The next highest European recipient of Chinese FDI is the United Kingdom for the sum of $330.33 million in 2010. Third, we note that the largest capital flows have gone to Virgin Islands ($6.12 billion), Cayman Islands ($34.96 billion), and Luxembourg ($3.2 billion), roughly 10 percent of the total capital outflow for that year. These countries are referred to as offshore financial centers (OFC) or tax havens.[1]

One explanation for the interesting phenomenon of large capital flows from China to the OFCs is that foreign private equity firms in China as well as Chinese firms transfer funds to offshore companies as special purpose vehicle enterprises in preparation for cross-border acquisitions or initial public offerings of shares of the Chinese enterprises worldwide, especially in those countries where high political constraints on FDI exist. Moreover, a change in the stock market regulation in Hong Kong in December 2009, allowed foreign companies including Virgin Islands based companies to list their stocks in Hong Kong Stock Exchange. Accordingly, Hong Kong Stock Exchange is used as an important channel

Table 14.2 Top five recipients of China's foreign direct investment by continents

Africa	Investment in 2010 (USD million)	Asia	Investment in 2010 (USD million)	Europe	Investment in 2010 (USD million)
South Africa	411.17	Singapore	1118.5	Luxembourg	3207.19
Democratic Republic of the Congo	236.19	Myanmar	875.61	Sweden	136.23
Niger	196.25	Thailand	699.87	Russian Federation	567.72
Algeria	186.00	Islamic Republic of Iran	511	Germany	412.35
Nigeria	184.89	Cambodia	466.51	Hungary	370.10
Total	2111.99		6385.25		6760.19
Latin America	Investment in 2010 (USD million)	North America	Investment in 2010 (USD million)	Oceania	Investment in 2010 (USD million)
Virgin Islands	6119.76	United States	2621.44	Australia	1701.7
Cayman Islands	3496.13	Canada	1142.29	New Zealand	63.75
Brazil	487.46	Bermuda	170.86	Fiji	5.57
Peru	139.03				
Venezuela	94.39				
Total	10538.27		2621.44		1888.96

Source: Ministry of Commerce, People's Republic of China (2013).

for foreign equity firms in China to transfer funds from Chinese financial market (Hempel and Gilbert 2010).

In addition to the increase in global and China's outward capital flow in recent decades, an increasing number of enterprises from the emerging market countries have become active in cross-border M&A activities beginning in the early 1990s. The emergence of these enterprises in the international M&A markets is motivated by the desire to achieve competitive advantage by acquiring resources such as natural resources, brands, technology, and management know-how. Because of the significant role China plays in the global economy, we focus on China's outbound M&A activities next.

Among those enterprises from the emerging markets, the Chinese enterprises, mostly state-owned enterprises (SOEs),[2] have become prominent players in the international M&A scene in recent years. It is reported that China's SOEs are responsible for four-fifth of the value of China's overseas acquisitions (Bradsher and De La Merced 2012).

The reasons for the prominent role of China's SOEs in foreign acquisitions include the size of acquiring firms (state enterprises are usually very large), government support of foreign acquisitions through preferential financing arrangement through state-owned banks, and profitability of SOEs (Song, Yang, and Zhang 2011).

Furthermore, China became the leading, by a wide margin, emerging market's foreign investor during these years. Moreover, as the data in Table 14.3 indicate, the value of total international M&As, both inbound and outbound, for Chinese enterprises has been increasing since 2007; however, even though the number of transactions has an upward trend, the value of the transactions declined in 2012.

Table 14.3 Number and value of international M&As by Chinese enterprises

	2007	2008	2009	2010	2011	2012
Number of deals	4,372	4,227	4,303	4,740	4,595	3,379
Value (USD billion)	103.5	138.7	199.7	221.6	225.0	307.79

Sources: Cai and Hu (2012).

In spite of the persistent rise in the value of China's international M&As,[3] the number of Chinese international M&A transactions has not increased continually. The rate of success[4] of international M&A bids of Chinese firms during 1982 to 2009 (a total of 1,324 acquisition attempts) is 51.2 percent compared to the success rate of U.S. firms (76.5 percent), and the worldwide average rate (68.7 percent), as well as that of some emerging countries, such as Brazil (70 percent), South Africa (72 percent), India (62.8 percent), and Russia (59 percent) during the same time span (Zhang and Ebbers 2010).

Geographic Distribution of Outbound Merger and Acquisition by Chinese Companies

According to survey results (Hasting 2013), three regions of the world are areas of top interest for China's outbound M&A activities. Investments in these regions include Asia-Pacific, Europe, and North America. Table 14.4 shows the geographic distribution of China's outbound M&A investment between 2011 and the fourth quarter of 2013.

According to the data in Table 14.4, the size of China's outbound investment in acquiring companies in Asia between 2011 and the end of 2013 remained relatively stable. However, one observes a reorientation of China's investment from North America to Europe during this period. The size of Chinese investment in North America has declined from 24 percent in 2011 to 17 percent in 2013, while China's investment in Europe has risen from 27 percent in 2011 to 36 percent in the first three quarters of 2013.

The decline in China's M&A activities in North America is partially due to publicly expressed national security concerns of both U.S. and

Table 14.4 Regional distribution of China's outbound M&As

Year	Asia	Europe	North America	Rest of the world
2013*	37%	36%	17%	10%
2012	34%	37%	20%	9%
2011	36%	27%	24%	13%

*Includes the first three quarters of 2013.
Source: Hastings (2013).

Canadian governments about foreign, including Chinese, acquisitions of enterprises in the critical industries of their respective countries (Squire Sanders Global M&A Briefing 2013).

Sectoral Focus of Outbound Merger and Acquisition by Chinese Companies

Energy and resource industries were the primary targets of interest for China's outbound M&As until the last few years. This is due to the rapid, persistent economic growth of China, and the adoption of a policy of reducing reliance on coal as a high carbon-based source of energy to reduce environmental pollution by the Chinese government. Additionally, in recent years Chinese enterprises have acquired companies producing consumer goods. The financial service sector is another target of interest for China's outbound M&As. Moreover, Chinese firms have shown interest in purchasing enterprises in leisure and entertainment, telecommunication, information technology, and transportation industries (Squire Sanders 2013).

Factors Contributing to Outbound Merger and Acquisition Activities by Chinese Enterprises

A review of the literature dealing with reasons for cross-border M&As reveals a number of motives that are common with domestic M&As including strategic moves (capture synergy, capitalize on company's core competency), entry into a new market, achieving economies of scale, and personal, that is, executive hubris and malfeasance. In addition to the listed motives for domestic M&As, cross-border M&As have another motive. Many corporate executives consider cross-border M&A as a method of diversification of risks associated with market volatility, and changes in governmental policies. Risk diversification is believed to increase innovation that is associated with cultural diversity, which promotes globalization synergies (Larsson and Finkelstein 1999; Olie 1990).

The ultimate goal of M&A transactions is capturing synergies that are to be found in combining the companies. Specifically, research shows the choice of M&A as a mode of entry into international markets is influenced by firm-level, industry-level, and country-level factors. Factors at the firm level consist of multinational and local experiences, product diversity, and international strategy. Industry-level variables include competitive capabilities such as technological intensity, advertising intensity, and sales force intensity. Finally, country-level factors consist of variables such as market growth in the host country, cultural differences between the home and host countries, and degree of risk aversion of the acquiring enterprise (Shimizu et al. 2004).

Recent surveys of Chinese executives, however, identify the specific motives by Chinese acquirers of foreign enterprises. For example, an event study by Boateng, Wang, and Yang (2008) using data from 27 Chinese cross-border M&A deals that took place by the purchase of stocks of target firms in the Shanghai and Shenzhen stock markets during 2000 to 2004, identifies the following strategic motives for the transactions that appear in Table 14.5.

Additionally, the findings of a survey of 100 executives from Greater China[5] who had engaged in outbound M&A activities identified the following top five motives for their acquisitions (Deloitte 2013).

- China's need for secure natural resources
- Continuing globalization of Chinese SOEs
- Euro zone sovereign debt crisis
- Renminbi internationalization
- Chinese government's *going-out policy*, which encourages outbound M&A activities of large Chinese enterprises by provision of bank financing for cross-border M&A transactions at preferential interest rates

Table 14.5 Motives for international M&A of Chinese enterprises

Motivation	Number	Percent
International expansion or diversification	17	39
Increase market share or power	12	27
Acquire strategic assets—technology, know-how, marketing	12	27
Overcome trade barriers	3	7

Source: Boateng, Wang, and Yang (2008).

It is also reported that for many Chinese overseas investments, high profits are not the main goal. The important motivating forces for China's outbound direct investment (ODI) including outbound M&As are acquiring technological capabilities of advanced economies and the natural resources of developing economies (Wang and Huang 2011).

The Role of Government and Information in Growth of Outbound Mergers and Acquisitions

Government regulations and cultural differences might have played important roles in further growth of Chinese outbound M&As. A recent opinion survey of 100 corporate executives, investment bankers, and private equity executives based in the United States and Greater China (Mainland, Hong Kong, Macao, and Taiwan), who had executive experiences in M&A transactions in entertainment, advertising, and digital media, showed that the respondents found government regulations the most significant obstacle in sustained growth of cross-border M&A activities in their industries (Manatt, Phelps & Phillips, LLP 2013). The second most important obstacle to further growth of M&A in these industries was information. The American executives perceived inadequate information for adequate due diligence of target firms in China a major issue. At the same time, the Chinese executives believed that Americans seek too much information when their enterprises wish to acquire a U.S.-based firm.

For example, an executive of a U.S. private equity firm based in Shanghai had the following comment concerning the Chinese view of American standard for transparency in M&As: "Disclosure requirements in the United States are not acceptable for Chinese companies, and the standards seem unnecessarily high. Sources of financing and long-term strategies are very confidential, and when this information is sought, deals tend to fail" (Manatt, Phelps & Phillips, LLP 2013, 17).

Even though these views were expressed by the executives in entertainment, advertising, and digital media, one could infer from them in general, American and Chinese executives in all industries share the same perceptions. These results have ramifications with respect to applicability of the procedures for M&As that were delineated in the earlier chapters of the book for outbound M&As by Chinese companies. Moreover, the obstacles seen by the Chinese executives perhaps are not confined to acquisitions in the United States. Perhaps, they have the same concerns about acquiring firms in other developed countries. In fact, our discussions of Chinese experiences in FDI in Australia (Chapter 5), and acquisition of a company in Italy (see Chapter 15) confirm the view expressed here.

The Role of Government of China in Outbound Merger and Acquisition Activities of Chinese Enterprises

Two sets of internal factors have shaped the policy of the government of China to promote M&A activities of select Chinese SOEs. The first factor is the existence of many large, inefficient, and monopolistic SOEs. These monopolies lack competition in internal markets and are protected by the government from international competition by virtue of being large SOEs. Therefore, these enterprises are content with the status quo of receiving support and privileges from the Chinese government, and have no incentive to gain competitive advantage on a global scale by acquiring technological and marketing capabilities. By following the policy of encouraging OFDI through M&As, the government of China aims to force the select monopolistic SOEs to become globally competitive. Internationalization of selective activities and industries in China is intended to promote value-chain upgrading and integration, acquiring access to and reducing the cost of raw materials, as well as acquiring tangible and intangible assets such as technology, brand names, and marketing capabilities (Sheng and Zhao 2013; Sauvant and Chen 2013).

The second factor is pressure by firms, most of which are private enterprises, which seek additional support from the Chinese government to promote OFDI through easier financing, research and development subsidies, stable fiscal policy, and human resource development (Sauvant and Chen 2013).

China's OFDI policy evolved in five stages since economic reforms in that country in 1979. These stages include (Huang and Austin 2011):

1. Gradual internationalization (1979 to 1985)

   During this phase, China formally recognized legality of international investment by allowing companies to establish offices and firms abroad. In 1983, the State Council established the Ministry of Foreign Trade and Economic Cooperation as the government agency in charge of OFDI.

2. Government encouragement of overseas direct foreign investment (1986 to 1990)

   During these years, the government actively encouraged overseas investment by Chinese SOEs.

3. Expansion and regulation (1991 to 1998)

   Due to a domestic surge in the inflation rate and a number of failed overseas investments, the Chinese authorities adopted policies to control overseas investments by SOEs in 1991. However, after the collapse of the former Soviet Union and economic liberalization in the Eastern European countries, mostly for political reasons, the State Council encouraged SOEs to trade with and invest in these countries in 1992.

4. Going-out period (1999 to 2001)

   This is the period in which China adopted a set of policies to encourage international investment, including establishing overseas processing and assembly operations of SOEs. The encouraging policies were mostly in response to the Asian Crisis of 1997 to 1999, during which China attempted to boost exports by relying on domestic low labor cost and less expensive overseas raw materials and energy resources. These policies set the stage for future development of Chinese OFDI.

5. The post-WTO (2002 to present) period

   In 2002, the government of China (State Council) emphasized the going-out strategy and considered it an important component of the overall long-run economic reform and liberalization policy of China. The policy statement further encouraged Chinese firms to invest overseas to gain technological and marketing capabilities and become globally competitive.

External Constraints for Chinese Mergers and Acquisitions

Chinese enterprises operating abroad face a number of challenges. These challenges include cultural distance, divergence between fields of competencies of merging companies, changing market conditions, and overoptimistic view of market size. We will discuss these issues in depth in the next chapter.

Summary

This chapter dealt with size and geographic distribution of Chinese OFDI including outbound M&As of Chinese enterprises. We discussed motivations for overseas acquisitions of China's SOEs and historical development of the Chinese government policy in promoting and encouraging outbound investment by Chinese enterprises.

CHAPTER 15

Major Issues in Chinese Cross-Border Mergers and Acquisitions

This chapter deals with China's rules and regulations governing the conduct of Chinese enterprises that aim to acquire foreign-owned enterprises abroad. We further discuss the accounting method for business combinations in China, review postmerger difficulties as well as integration challenges of the Chinese enterprises that invested abroad, and examine policies of the United States and Australia with respect to China's direct investment in those countries.

An Overview of Merger and Acquisition Process in China

Chinese enterprises that aim to acquire target companies abroad must comply with certain rules and regulations in China to obtain license from China's government for the acquisition. In the following, we discuss the main government agencies that are responsible for management of cross-border acquisitions by Chinese enterprises.

Rules for Overseas Acquisitions by Chinese Enterprises

Chinese regulations require that four different agencies approve each overseas acquisition. These agencies include: State Council, the National Development and Reform Commission (NDRC), the Ministry of Commerce (MOFCOM), and the State Administration of Foreign Exchange Control (SAFE).

In certain cases, permission for financial and banking investment from sector-specific regulators such as the China Banking Regulatory Commission and the China Insurance Regulatory Commission is also required. Outbound investments by state-owned enterprises (SOEs) require approval by the State-owned Assets Supervision and Administration Commission of the State Council (SASAC), which at its central level supervises 117 SOEs.[1] In some cases, review by the People's Republic of China's (PRC) antitrust regulators may also be required.

If extra financing or a fast approval process in certain sectors (such as clean energy) is required, then the approval of the Ministry of Industry and Information Technology is also needed.

The Measures for the Administration of Outbound Investments (the Outbound Investment Measures), which became effective on May 1, 2009, defines an outbound investment as any transaction that establishes "a new overseas enterprise, the merger with or acquisition of an existing overseas enterprise, or obtaining control rights or business management rights thereof" (Wang et al. 2009).

State Council

The State Council of the PRC, which is also known as the Central People's Government, is the highest executive authority and state administration of the country. The State Council, among its other administrative duties, mandates the NDRC, which relies on its Department of Foreign Capital and Overseas Investment, for "....examining and approving key foreign-invested projects, major resources related overseas investment projects and projects that consume substantial amount of foreign currency" (NDRC 2014).

The Role of National Development and Reform Commission (NDRC)

The NDRC is the main government agency that designs, regulates, and coordinates national economic development and industrial policy of the PRC. In addition to overseeing government investments in the domestic economy of China, the Department of Foreign Capital and Overseas

Investment of NDRC adopts "strategies, goals and policies to balance and optimize China's overseas investments" (Wenbin and Wilkes 2011, 4).

Any outbound investment by Chinese enterprises must first be reviewed by NDRC. Before any overseas acquisitions, a Chinese private or state-owned enterprise must obtain a letter of approval to be submitted to the other state agencies that are responsible for management and control of foreign direct investment (FDI) of China's enterprises. In general, based on Administrative Measures for Examination and Approval of Overseas Investment Projects, which was published on August 16, 2012, the NDRC and its offices are responsible for reviewing all investment projects that fall into the following two categories:

1. Outlays exceeding $300 million in resource-based sectors
2. Outlays exceeding $100 million in nonresource-based sectors
   Review of investment less than the above stated minimum threshold is the responsibility of NDRC's local offices.

Nonetheless, on December 2, 2013, the Chinese central government (State Council) announced that only investments over $1 billion or investments involving sensitive countries, regions, or industries will require NDRC approval, even though all investments between $300 million and $1 billion are required to be filed with NDRC in all cases (Xiong, Schroder, and Tudor 2014). Contrary to the final project approval regime by the NDRC process, filing an investment in sensitive countries and industries does not require an in-depth review of the project, and is considered "preliminary review".

Overseas investment projects must meet a number of conditions including compliance with the laws and regulations of China; compliance with the sustainable development of the economy; promotion of exports of technology, products, and services; and compliance with national capital projects and foreign loans. The applicants must also demonstrate their financial capability to invest in the proposed project.

Before a formal review process, a prereview examination of the project is required by NDRC. All Chinese enterprises wishing to invest overseas are required to receive a confirmation letter from the NDRC by submitting a report to NDRC describing the project before any executable binding agreements, proposing binding offers, applying to the foreign government authorities, and launching official bids.

The authority of the NDRC applies not only to direct foreign investment, but also to indirect foreign investment, in the form of providing financing or guarantees to another entity or for the benefit of the offshore affiliates of Chinese enterprises.

Ministry of Commerce (MOFCOM)

MOFCOM oversees the establishment of newly formed enterprises that were acquired through cross-border mergers and acquisitions (M&As). The supervision includes reviewing major agreements, contracts, and documents, for example, review of articles of association of the enterprises to be established. After approving an application for cross-border M&A, the ministry issues the Certificate of Enterprises' Outbound Investment to the applicant.

The following categories of cross-border investment require approval by the MOFCOM.

- Investments in countries that have no diplomatic relationships with China
- Investments in certain countries, which may involve "political sensitivity," require review by MOFCOM and the Ministry of Foreign Affairs
- Investments in excess of $100 million
- Investments involving more than one country or region
- Investments involving the establishment of overseas special purpose vehicles (SPVs)

State Administration of Foreign Exchange (SAFE)

SAFE is the Chinese government agency that is responsible for controlling China's foreign exchange transactions. After the approval of an application for a cross-border investment by NDRC and MOFCOM, another application must be filed with the SAFE for a Foreign Exchange Registration Certificate of Outbound Direct Investment. In the past, this step also involved another review and approval; however, in recent years, this application is a mere registration requirement.

Recent Developments in China's Outbound Investment Policy Regarding SOEs

The SASAC is a government agency that is in charge of management of Chinese SOEs. SASAC "…performs investor's responsibilities, supervises and manages the state-owned assets of the enterprises under the supervision of the Central Government (excluding financial enterprises), and enhances the management of the state-owned assets" (SASAC 2014). Created in 2003, SASAC manages nonfinancial SOEs according to the principle of separation of government administration from enterprise management, by separating management and ownership of the enterprises.

Both the national government and the provincial governments manage SOEs through SASACs. The national government has 117 central SASACs and the provincial SOEs are managed by Provincial SASAC. The organizational flowchart of SOEs in China appears in Figure 15.1.

As depicted in the flowchart the Central SASAC directly reports to State Council, and the government exercises its ownership control of SOEs by appointment of board members and approval of appointment of senior executives of the enterprises. Moreover, the Organization Department of Communist Party of China plays a role in the management of central SOEs by influencing the appointment of senior management of the enterprises.

Finally, central and provincial SOEs can have wholly, partially owned subsidiaries, or both as well as can enter into joint ventures with foreign or private domestic enterprises (Larum and Qian 2012).

In 2011, the SASAC published two new rules that were to govern the conduct of SOEs or their subsidiaries in outbound investment activities. The first rule is called *Interim measures for the supervision and administration of overseas State-owned assets of central State-owned Enterprises* (Rule 26). The second rule is *Interim measures for the administration of overseas property rights of State-owned Enterprises* (Rule 27). These rules became effective on July 1, 2011. Additionally Circular 114, which further recognized and enhanced SOE's overseas property rights, was issued by the SASAC and became effective on September 29, 2011. The rules and circular were applicable to enterprises under the jurisdiction of the

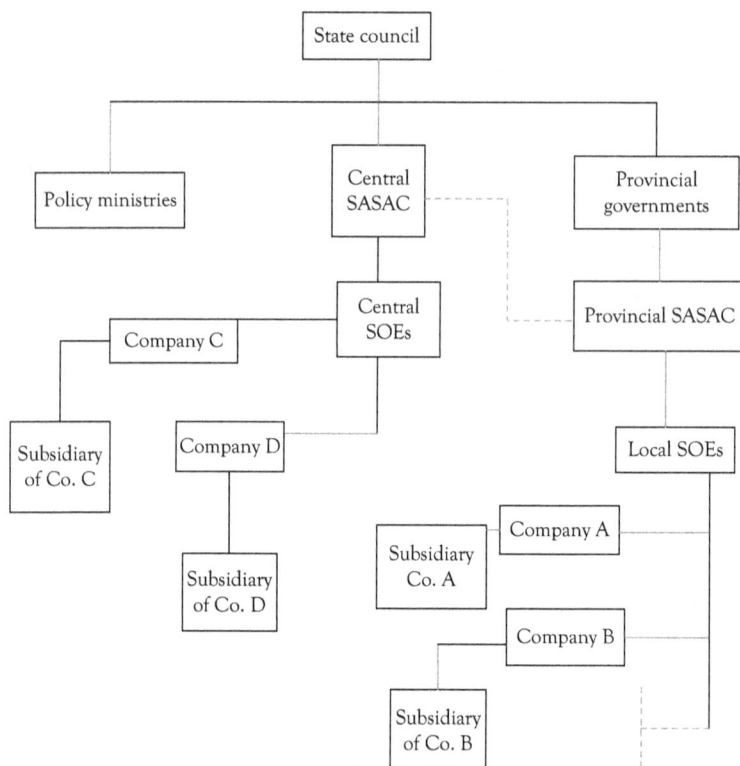

Figure 15.1 Organizational flowchart of central and provincial SASAC and SOEs

Source: Larum and Qian (2012).

central-level SASAC; however, the provincial-level SASAC has followed suit. Approval of the SASAC is required only in cases where overseas investment falls outside of the primary business of the acquiring SOE, even though approval from NDRC, MOFCOM, and SAFE for these SOEs is required (Norton Rose Fulbright 2014).

We discuss the requirements of the rules next.[2]

Approval and Filing Requirements

According to Article 7 of Rule 26, merger or acquisition of an overseas listed company, or any "material" overseas investment by a central SOE or its major subsidiary, must be filed with or receive approval from the SASAC. The filing should include information on the size of overall investment, source and composition of funds used on offshore investments. Moreover, the filing should include information regarding the investment projects, containing data such as, the background of investment, description of the investment project, capital structure, investment location and size, financing plan, the implementing terms, risk analysis, and investment cash flows.

Due Diligence

Article 8 of Rule 26 requires due diligence for all overseas investments.

Valuation

Article 9 of Rule 27 requires that in all cases where an SOE intends to use onshore state-owned assets for overseas investments, or transfer the sum of money equal to the appraised asset value to another entity, the appraisal must be conducted by a domestic valuation institution. The appraisal must be filed at the SASAC for approval .

Article 6 of Circular 114 mandates an appraisal of the value of overseas assets to be purchased or sold by a central SOE by a professional appraisal institution with the necessary qualification and good reputation as well as expertise. Article 6 of Circular 114 is applicable to those investments by noncash asset means of payment or changes in holding of shares in nonlisted companies by central SOEs and their subsidiaries.

Article 10, Rule 27, requires that central SOE file appraisal and obtain approval from the SASAC in the event of any transactions by the SOE, which could result in a reduction of state ownership.

All transactions must be based on the appraised value of the assets.

Financing

Article 22, Rule 26, prohibits offshore SOEs and their subsidiaries, with the exception of offshore state-owned financial institutions, from providing financing of any kind to any individual or entity that is not a member of the same group.

Registration and Monitoring of Overseas State-Owned Assets

Article 8, Rule 27, mandates that any overseas acquired state-owned assets and any change in overseas state-owned assets should be registered with the SASAC. Furthermore, Article 4, Circular 114, requires that annual report covering the administration of overseas state-owned properties be submitted to the SASAC by April 30 each year.

Special Purpose Vehicles

Article 11, Rule 26, pertains to registration and approval of SPVs[3], and sale of offshore state-owned assets. According to the article, the decision to set up an offshore SPV by the central SOE must be reported to the SASAC in writing. Any SPVs that do not perform useful function must be dissolved. If the payment for the sale of offshore assets is not to be received in one lump sum, the buyer must provide security guaranteeing the outstanding payments.

Recent Development of Chinese Government Regulation of Outbound Investment of China's Enterprises

Given the growing interest on the part of China's enterprises for outbound acquisitions, the PRC MOFCOM, as the leading market regulatory agency of China, issued three administrative provisions, guidelines, and policies relating to cross-border M&A activities of China's enterprises in late March and early April of 2013. These measures encourage outbound acquisitions by Chinese enterprises so long as the investments meet the principles of equity, fairness, and generally acceptable commercial practices. The MOFCOM directives promote fair competition and prohibit unfair business practices, require adoption of environment-friendly policies of acquiring companies, and set standard practices to be used by the ministry's units and functionaries as well as for Chamber of Commerce and other organizations that are concerned with FDI.

The MOFCOM defines unfair competition to mean any of the following forms of conduct: acquiring business opportunities by bribery; adopting unfair, cut-throat pricing policies; engaging in collusive agreements; damaging the business reputation of a competitor; having false claims to achievements of one's own enterprise; false advertising, and other activities which are considered unfair competition in law.

To ensure accountability on the part of outbound investors regarding their business conduct, the MOFCOM intends to establish a "bad credit filing system" of overseas investment. The system will aim to record the unfair and anticompetitive conduct of Chinese enterprises that invest abroad and report any misbehavior by these entities to the relevant authorities and institutions. All Chinese enterprises with a bad credit record will be excluded from receiving any policy support from the government of the PRC for 3 years.

The content of the guidelines spells out the social responsibility of enterprises, and makes implementation of the responsibility mandatory for China's enterprises that invest overseas. These responsibilities include: adopting environment- friendly policies by observing the environmental laws and regulations of the host country as well as standards and practices adopted by international organizations; showing sensitivity to and paying respect to religious beliefs and customs of host countries; and protecting the rights and interests of local workers.

Finally the internal standard practices recommended by MOFCOM aim at the establishment of efficient, transparent corporate governance of Chinese overseas' enterprises by the mechanism of increased inspection of these enterprises. These measures should be similar to those policies adopted by developed countries, countries that were successful in preventing commercial bribery and in promoting efficient, transparent corporate governance. Furthermore, the standards aim to create corporate culture within Chinese enterprises abroad; promote the public image of Chinese companies; strengthen regulation of overseas Chinese enterprises; and insist on the implementation of the Regulation on the Administration of Foreign Labor Cooperation (Wu 2013).

Accounting Method for Business Combinations in China

Accounting for the proposed M&A constitutes an important part of financial analysis in M&A decision making. In China, the rules for Generally

Accepted Accounting Practices, PRC GAAP, were issued by Ministry of Finance under Accounting Standard for Business Combination, No. 20, in 2006.

Accounting Standards for Enterprises No. 20—Business Combinations defines business combination as follows: "The term 'business combinations' refers to a transaction or event bringing together two or more separate enterprises into one reporting entity. Business combinations are classified into the business combinations under the same control and the business combinations not under the same control." Moreover, business combination under the same control is defined as "…. a business combination in which all of the combining enterprises are ultimately controlled by the same party" (Kuai 2006). Accordingly, one can construe a business combination of two or more entities that are under the same control as an M&A.

This rule essentially converges with international business combination standards. The rule requires the use of the "pooling-of-interest method" for business combinations involving entities under common control.

Postmerger Integration Experiences of Chinese Enterprises

In Chapter 13, we discussed postmerger integration processes of private enterprises in great detail. However, discussing whether Chinese enterprises follow the same practices as described in that chapter would be insightful. We will discuss postmerger integration practices of Chinese acquiring firms by reviewing some of China's FDI post merger practices in Australia and by examining two case studies of Chinese acquisitions in Italy and the United States. Selection of the Australian experiences is motivated by the rising Chinese FDI in that country, which has caused a surge in Australian nationalistic reactions to Chinese investments, restrictions on Chinese FDI in the country, and complaints of Australian discriminatory practices against Chinese firms by China (Mendelshon and Fels 2013). The case in the United States exemplifies inadequate legal due diligences, and the Italian case demonstrates insufficient post-merger integration.

Overseas Investment Performances of Chinese State-Owned Enterprises

Observations of cross-border, postmerger experiences of many Chinese firms indicate that Chinese enterprises operating abroad have not been very effective in adopting new technology, in creating new brands, in investing in marketing and intangible assets, and in adopting Western management practices and corporate governance standards and regulations (Spigarelli, Alon, and Mucelli 2013). Studies have shown that "....in the past 20 years, 67% of China's cross-border M&A have not been successful and almost all of the country's technology-seeking M&A have failed" (Chen and Wang 2012, 282).

Factors that contribute to postmerger failure of newly formed enterprises include, but are not limited to (Deloitte 2011; Chen and Wang 2012):

1. Changing market conditions
2. Optimistic view of the market size
3. Selecting an unsuitable partner or having incorrect focus
4. Cultural differences
5. Poor leadership
6. Acquiring an enterprise that is too far removed from the core competency of the acquiring firm

In what follows, we aim to identify additional factors that might be contributing to the not too successful outcomes by case studies.

Due Diligence and Chinese Acquisitions in Australia, Italy and the United States

Anecdotal experiences of Chinese acquiring companies in Australia and the United States, which we discussed earlier in the book confirm the difficulties Chinese entities face in the due diligence stage of acquiring companies abroad. The problems faced by CITIC Pacific and Ralls Corporation, which were discussed in case studies in Chapter 5, are notable examples that may have resulted from inadequate due diligence. In the CITIC Pacific case, even though the initial investment in acquiring the target was $4.2 billion, by the time of production of the output in July 2011, the total investment by CITIC was estimated to have reached $5.2 billion (Sun, Zhang, Chen, 2013; Huang and Austin 2011). In the Ralls Corporation case, the company was forced to cease construction and operating activities and was forbidden to divest without permission of CFIUS. In what follows we will examine two additional cases , which involve Chinese acquisitions in Italy and the United States. The new case studies allow drawing important lessons for appreciation of importance of sufficient legal and cultural due diligences in M&A's.

China's Acquisitions in Australia

The pattern of postacquisition integration processes of Chinese acquiring companies in seven acquisitions in Australia indicates a mixed approach in terms of retaining or dismissing the top executives of the acquired companies. The experiences of Chinese acquisitions in Australia show that transferring executives from the acquiring companies to the target depends on the international experiences of the acquiring companies: The higher the international experience of the acquirer, the higher the likelihood of replacing the top management of the target with the executives of the acquiring firm. For example, both Sinosteel and CITIC Pacific appointed their managing director and executive chairman to their Australian subsidiaries, Sinosteel Midwest Corporation and CITIC Pacific Mining, respectively. However, the Chinese enterprises with less international experience retained the executives of the acquired Australian firms and also transferred some of their own executives to the target companies (Huang and Austin 2011).

China's Acquisition in Italy

Case Study: Qianjiang Motors Acquires Benelli Motorcycles

We use a case study presented by Spigarelli, Alon, and Mucelli (2013) to illustrate the cultural challenges faced in postacquisition integration process by a Chinese acquirer.

Qianjiang Motors, a Chinese SOE, which is located in Zhejiang province in Southeast China, is a manufacturer of motorcycles and engine parts among other products. The company has 7 percent of the market share in China and exports to more than 110 countries. The target company, Benelli Motorcycles, is a small, family-owned Italian manufacturer of motorcycles and scooters that was established in 1911. The Italian company was started as a repair shop for automobile and motorcycles, which also manufactured automobile parts. Having acquired technical know-how, the firm introduced one of its manufactured motorcycles at the Third International Bicycle and Motorcycle Exhibition in Milan in 1921. Winning many national and international awards for manufacturing and design excellence, the firm became very successful in the European market. However, the success of the company ended in the 1960s when Japanese-manufactured motorcycles entered the European and world markets. By 2005, the company had to cease production because of loss of the market share and massive financial losses. The company went bankrupt in 2005.

The Chinese SOE acquired the Italian firm in September 2005, and the combined operations began a month later in October. Given the technical know-how and advanced design skills of the Italian firm, the Chinese company's goal to acquire it was based on its strategic move to access the technical capabilities of the target. Additionally, the Italian company enjoyed a reputable brand name. The acquirer's strategy was to combine the technical and marketing capabilities of the Italian company with its own favorable cost of production so that it could compete with the Japanese producers of motorcycles globally.

The location of Benelli Motorcycles is in a province in Italy where the local government and trade unions are very involved in economic activities, and they played an important role in completing the deal.

In the postacquisition phase, the Chinese acquiring company restructured the production processes to increase efficiency, raise production capacity, and by doing so lowered the costs of production. The new entity planned to double the workforce and introduce six products within 2 years. However, no major change in administration was planned. Only the sales director, the part quality manager, and the managing director were relocated from China to Italy. Despite the minimal changes in the management of the target firm, several post-merger integration issues including national cultural differences with respect to attitudes, lifestyles, and approaches to business management appeared.

Using the sales revenues as a measure of postmerger performance of the new company shows that acquisition was not totally successful. In spite of more or less steady sales of the rivals, the new company's products sold in Italy dropped from 848 in 2008 to 163 in 2009. Specifically, the total value of production of the acquired company dropped from 13.972 million euros in 2006 (the year after acquisition) to 7.747 million euros in 2010. Nevertheless, while both the debts and assets of the company decreased, its equity increased between 2006 and 2010 (Spigarelli, Alon, and Mucelli 2013).

Moreover, difficulties in coordination of human resources mostly in the form of communication because of languages, cultural background, and work habits delayed the development of new products. English was used as a language of communication, but neither side was proficient in English. The Chinese would speak in Mandarin during official meetings on occasions where the two sides disagreed on certain issues. In such conditions, building trust became very challenging.

The differences between Chinese and Italians on the issue of belonging and work habits created another challenge. The Chinese showed a strong commitment to the success of the company, and were willing to work at evenings and weekends; the Italians found such work habits unacceptable, even under urgent situations.

Differences between Chinese and Italian executives on policies such as expenditure of resources for image of the firm, advertising, and customer cares also created friction. The Chinese did not place these items on the top of the priority list, while the Italian executives considered them to be very important. Moreover, persistent efforts on the part of Chinese executives to reduce costs resulted in delays in investments.

The accounting and management information systems of the two companies were not integrated. Finally, the hierarchy, line of command, and responsibility of human resources were not well-defined, and the power was mostly at the disposal of the managing director.

China's Acquisitions in the United States

Case Study: Lenovo Acquires IBM's PC Division

In 2005, Lenovo, a Chinese computer company, acquired IBM's per-
sonal-computer division. Lenovo's strategy for the acquisition of IBM
PC division, as stated by Liu Chuanzhi, the founder and chairman
of Legend Holding Ltd was capturing synergies from "...leveraging
Lenovo's strength in China and IBM PCs strength in advanced
countries, integrating procurement capabilities, optimizing supply
relationships, and streamlining end-to-end processes from order taking
through fulfillment, all contributing to become more efficient" (Rui
and Yip 2008, 220). The motive for Lenovo's globalization efforts in
spite of its preeminence in China's personal computer (PC) market,
which emerged from the company's competitive advantages such as its
technological advantage in China's niche PC market over its foreign
competitors, its large market share, and its profitability in China is
based on the potential threat the foreign competitors posed for Lenovo.
Both Dell and Hewlett Packard were acquiring more knowledge of the
Chinese local market.[4]

Qiao Song, Lenovo's senior vice president and chief procurement
officer, was assigned the task of the rapid integration of the purchasing
departments of IBM PC division and Lenovo, departments that had
different processes, management systems, and cultures. Three months
before the closing date, the top management of Lenovo also mandated
that Mr. Qiao Song save the merged companies over $150 million in
direct spending on materials and show an overall annual saving of $300
million within 18 months after closing. Mr. Song met and exceeded
the target cost reduction by creating a general-procurement function for
the company that was responsible for managing overheads, expenditure
such as travels and office supplies. How did Mr. Qiao Song achieve his
goal?

In an interview given to McKinsey & Company in May 2008,
Mr. Qiao Song (Hexter 2008) stated that in spite of vast differences
between the two purchasing departments, the purchasing teams of both
companies considered full integration of the purchasing departments to

be a top priority because of the sum of money that was to be saved. The managers of the purchasing departments realized that the system differences included processes, information technology (IT), management systems, key performance indicators, and cultures. Given such incongruities, the first set of tasks was determining the production costs for each company, identifying the immediate saving opportunities after closing, and integrating the purchasing departments.

One of the first tasks was identification of costs of the companies. Due to legal restrictions during the negotiations, direct comparison of costs was not permitted. The companies had to select certain members from both purchasing departments so that they could review and analyze cost data for both companies. During these review sessions, the combined team was able to identify common supply categories where Lenovo could share supplies with IBM. Next, synergies from Lenovo's newly found global access to supplies were realized.

The third source of cost saving was reduction of material costs by redesigning products or eliminating internal items in the products that were not valued by customers. Cost structures of all products of the new company were analyzed. The idea behind such examination was to determine whether a new product design was required or in some cases whether the excessive specifications for a product, for example, internal items that customers could not see, value, or were willing to pay were to be eliminated. Moreover, the process allowed standardization of products, which allowed the company to realize synergy from economies of scale by increasing the volume of purchases from some suppliers.

The net effect of these per-closing costs of production analyses was that the new Lenovo company had a clear understanding of the savings they needed to get, the methods they had to adopt to get them, and the time it required to obtain the savings.

Mr. Qiao Song described the cultural differences between IBM and Lenovo by stating that Lenovo had an entrepreneurial culture, while IBM's culture was very systematic and analytical. Moreover, on the issue of overcoming cultural differences between the management teams of IBM and Lenovo, Mr. Song indicated that the balance between flexibility in dealing with the senior executives who had difficulties adapting to change during the initial adjustment period and firmness on the performance results was the key to success. He stated that accommodating the senior executives during the adjustment period was fruitful and resulted in complete acculturation and fine performance of those executives. He went on to say that he was focused on results and after the closing of the deal he had a bimonthly review for each product. He required the team members to report on their cost saving efforts. One of the areas that Mr. Song found great resistance from IBM executives was air travel expenses that they thought were very personal. Mr. Song solved the travel expenditure issue by relying on credible insiders who were very familiar with the issue rather than relying on outside consultants to remedy the problem.

Further examination of Lenovo Group's culture is helpful in developing an understanding of how cultural differences in cross-border M&As could pose difficulties in integration processes.

It is instructive to discuss the pivotal role Mr. Yang Yuanqing played in the development of Lenovo. Mr. Yang, an engineer by training, is the chief executive officer of Lenovo Group, a company that had a humble beginning in 1984. Mr. Yang is described to have a "forceful personality" and is an unrepentant believer in discipline and centralized decision making (Stahl and Köster 2013). Following his disciplinarian instinct, President Yang required that all employees of the company abide by the following company rules:

1. Treat customers and suppliers with care and respect
2. Be frugal: "save money, save energy, save time"
3. Concentrate on the fundamental leadership tasks: build the management team, develop strategy, and lead the employees
4. Do not abuse your position to benefit yourself
5. Do not accept bribes
6. Do not take second employment
7. Do not share information about your salary with your coworkers
8. All employees had to use time clock to check in and out
9. Employees who were tardy to meetings had to stand behind their chair for one minute
10. All employees who were found outside the office building without a reasonable explanation received pay dock[5]

One could easily imagine that enforcing these rules in Lenovo operations in the United States or other Western countries would pose formidable challenges for the management, because workers in Western countries are resistant to a rigid work environment.

Lenovo is a global player in the IT industry and has become the number one producer of PCs globally. We present the following interesting stories about the company to learn about some recent developments pertaining to Lenovo, and its strategy to become a global entity through M&As.

Bloomberg Technology reported on September 2, 2013, that Chief Executive Officer Yang Yuanqing will share $3.25 million of his bonus with workers for a second year. Lenovo's staff totaling 10,000 workers in 20 countries received payments in September 2013, in recognition of their contributions to the company. About 85 percent of the recipients are in China (Bloomberg 2013).

Benevolence of Lenovo's chief executive in contrast to practices of some executives of U.S. companies demanding wage and benefit concessions from employees in the midst of high profitability, while at the same time awarding themselves hefty salary raises and bonuses (Greenhouse 2012) is another clear evidence of the cultural differences between the companies.

On January 20, 2014, *Bloomberg Businessweek* (Culpan 2014) reported that Lenovo Business Group Ltd is in serious negotiations in acquiring IBM's low-end server division. The report indicates that Lenovo has completed due diligence and trying to diversify into the server business because of falling demand for PCs. IBM plans to spin off the unit because of its lower profit margin.

According to an e-mail message received by one of the authors from Thomas F. Looney, vice president and general manager, Lenovo North America, Lenovo will acquire:

- IBM's x86 product lines (including towers, racks, blades, and high-density systems)
- All blade networking technology products
- Solutions and converged systems tied to the previously-mentioned products

- All associated intellectual property (IP)
- IBM's x86 sales force, research and development teams, quality and product assurance engineers, key labs and other facilities supporting these products

On January 29, 2014, it was announced that Lenovo is in negotiations with Google to acquire Motorola Mobility smartphone business for an initial negotiating price offer of $2.91 billion. With a fast growing smartphone business, the acquisition if completed will give Lenovo a strong position in North and Latin Americas, and a stepping stone into Western Europe. These new markets would complement Lenovo's smartphone business in the emerging markets. According to the proposed offer, Lenovo will pay $1.41 billion, consisting of $660 million in cash and $750 million in Lenovo's common stocks, at closing. The remaining balance of $1.5 billion will be paid by a 3-year promissory note (Lenovo 2014).

Policies of Governments of the Host Countries Toward Chinese Outbound Direct Investment

The experiences of many Chinese companies in acquiring companies in North America and Australia have not always been pleasant and positive. In fact, due to the inexperience of many Chinese enterprises in conduct of international business, particularly in M&As, the outbound investing Chinese enterprises have paid heavily for their mistakes. Due to the importance of these experiences for future outbound direct investment including M&A activities of Chinese firms, we will discuss governmental policies and Chinese investment practices in Australia and the United States next.

United States' Policy Toward Foreign Acquisitions of American Companies and Chinese Experiences of Acquisitions in the United States

The policy of the U.S. government concerning foreign acquisitions of enterprises in the United States is governed by Foreign Investment and National Security Act of 2007. The law defines "covered transaction" to mean "…any merger, acquisition, or takeover that is proposed or pending after August 23, 1988, by or with any foreign person which could result in foreign control of any person engaged in interstate commerce in the United States." Furthermore, "the term 'foreign government-controlled transaction' means any covered transaction that could result in the control of any person engaged in interstate commerce in the United States by a foreign government or an entity controlled by or acting on behalf of a foreign government" (United States of America 2007, 246–247).

In the United States, the trigger for review of the proposed merger is set in motion if the proposed acquisition is in high technology firms, in sectors of critical infrastructure, or if it may result in significant outsourcing of jobs.

The critical infrastructure sectors of the economy include most of the major sectors of the economy including the following: chemical; communication; commercial facilities; critical manufacturing; dams; defense industrial base; emergency services; energy; financial services; food and agriculture; government facilities; healthcare; public health; IT; nuclear reactors, materials, and waste; transportation systems; and water and waste water systems (Department of Homeland Security 2013).

It should be noted that other advanced industrial countries have a similar set of policies concerning foreign acquisitions of domestic enterprises, particularly acquisitions of firms in the critical infrastructure sectors. For discussions of how different countries define critical infrastructure and a short history of the development of laws for control of FDI in the United States, see Masters (2013).

Committee on Foreign Investment in the United States (CFIUS)

As discussed in previous chapters, the Committee on Foreign Investment in the United States (CFIUS) has the responsibility of reviewing M&As of foreign enterprises in the United States, and report to the president of the United States those mergers or acquisitions that are potential threats to the national security of the United States (see Chapter 5 for the case study involving Ralls Corporation and CFIUS). The CFIUS must issue an annual report to the U.S. Congress on the number of notices submitted by foreign enterprises that planned to acquire American companies, the number of filings that were investigated, and the number of filings that were withdrawn.

According to the 2012 Annual Report issued by CFIUS (2014), there were 23 filings by Chinese acquiring companies in 2012, which showed a dramatic rise in such filings by Chinese entities. This number compares to 10 filings in 2011 and 6 filings in 2010. According to this report, Chinese investors had the highest number of filings among 21 foreign investors who filed with CFIUS to declare their intention to acquire companies in the United States. The top five foreign investors were from China (23), United Kingdom (17), Canada (13), Japan (9), and France (8). In addition to China, three were from BRICS (Brazil, Russia, India, China, South Africa) countries including India (4), Brazil (2), and Russian Federation (2).

The committee reports that 45 out of 114 filers in 2012 were investigated; however, it does not publicly report the nationality of the applicants who were investigated. Nevertheless, the published data show that in spite of a 26 percent decline in the number of companies filing for authorization to acquire a target company in the United States, the number and percentage of the applications that were investigated by CFIUS are on the rise (see Table 15.1).

Table 15.1 Total filing, number, and percentage of investigations by CFIUS

Year	Number of notices	Number of investigations	Percentage of investigations
2008	155	23	15.00
2009	65	25	38.00
2010	93	35	38.00
2011	111	40	36.00
2012	114	45	39.00

Source: CFIUS (2014).

Does CFIUS Place Chinese Acquiring Companies Under Special Scrutiny?

Given that the data for the number of investigations by nationality of applicants are not publicly available, one cannot make a factual statement about whether CFIUS places the Chinese filers under special scrutiny. Nonetheless, the CFIUS went on record stating in its 2011 Annual Report that "Based on its assessment of transactions identified by CFIUS for purposes of this report, the U.S. Intelligence Community (USIC) judges with moderate confidence that there is likely a coordinated strategy among one or more foreign governments or companies to acquire U.S. companies involved in research, development, or production of critical technologies for which the United States is a leading producer" (CFIUS 2012, 23). Even though the CFIUS did not report a "coordinated strategy" by any government or company owned by a foreign government to acquire company with a "critical technology" during 2012, there is circumstantial evidence that CFIUS views investors from countries that are not allies of the United States with caution.

In addition to the data on a simultaneous rise in the number of filings by investors from BRICS countries and an increase in the number of cases CFIUS reviewed,[6] we present the view of a U.S. law firm that specializes in representing companies in M&A matters. In support of the presence of the cautionary approach by CFIUS in dealing with foreign acquisitions from the BRICS countries, particularly from China, we cite a commentary by a U.S. law firm, which states that "...our observation of CFIUS reactions to China-related cases continues to suggest that CFIUS views China and countries that are known to have close economic and military ties to China with heightened suspicion in terms of their potential to execute coordinated strategies to acquire leading-edge U.S. technologies. CFIUS is likely to be particularly sensitive with respect to transactions involving Chinese government-owned or affiliated acquirers. However, even where subjected to heightened scrutiny, China-related transactions have continued to be approved by CFIUS" (Latham & Watkins 2014, 2). Moreover, the 2012 Annual Report stated a number of factors it considered in its review of covered transactions. We quote these considerations from the 2012 Annual Report.

Foreign control of U.S. businesses that:

- Provide products and services to an agency or agencies of the U.S. government, or state and local authorities that have functions that are relevant to national security
- Provide products or services that could expose national security vulnerabilities, including potential cyber security concerns, or create vulnerability to sabotage or espionage. This includes consideration of whether the covered transaction will increase the risk of exploitation of the particular U.S. business's position in the supply chain
- Have operations, or produce or supply products or services, the security of which may have implications for U.S. national security, such as businesses that involve infrastructure that may constitute critical infrastructure; businesses that involve various aspects of energy production, including extraction, generation, transmission, and distribution; businesses that affect the national transportation system; and businesses that could significantly and directly affect the U.S. financial system
- Have access to classified information or sensitive government or government contract information, including information about employees
- Are in the defense, security, and national security related law enforcement sectors
- Are involved in activities related to weapons and munitions manufacturing, aerospace, satellite, and radar systems
- Produce certain types of advanced technologies that may be useful in defending, or in seeking to impair, U.S. national security, which may include businesses engaged in the design and production of semiconductors and other equipment or components that have both commercial and military applications, or the design, production, or provision of goods and services involving network and data security
- Engage in the research and development, production, or sale of technology, goods, software, or services that are subject to U.S. export controls

- Are in proximity to certain types of United States Government USG facilities

The Report stated the following additional considerations.

Acquisition of control by foreign persons who:

- Are controlled by a foreign government
- Are from a country with a record on nonproliferation and other national security related matters that raises concerns
- Have a historical record of taking or intentions to take actions that could impair U.S. national security (CFIUS 2014, 22–23)

The preceding discussions clearly point to the need for complete legal due diligence by Chinese enterprises before any attempts to negotiate with target companies in the United States.

The U.S. Securities Laws and Acquisition of U.S. Public Companies

In addition to the direct control of foreign acquisitions of U.S.-based companies, the government of the United States has rules and regulations that aim to protect public interest by regulating sales of securities to the public. Prominent among the federal securities laws is the Securities and Exchange Commission (SEC) Act of 1934, which created the SEC. The SEC is to enforce the securities laws and regulate sales and purchases of securities in the United States. The SEC Act requires "… disclosure of important information by anyone seeking to acquire more than 5 percent of a company's securities by direct purchase or tender offer. Such an offer often is extended in an effort to gain control of the company" (Securities and Exchange Commission 2014).

Foreign enterprises that acquire publicly listed companies in the United States, or list their shares in the U.S. stock exchanges may be audited by the SEC or the Public Company Accounting Oversight Board (PCAOB). The PCAOB is the enforcement arm of the Sarbanes–Oxley Act of 2002, which was legislated after fraudulent practices of a number of large U.S.-based corporations that led to their bankruptcy and massive financial losses by the investing public. Among other issues surrounding the Saranes-Oxley Act, PCAOB auditing, on occasions, have led to the conflict of U.S. securities laws and the laws of the country of the company, which lists shares in U.S. exchanges (Walker 2005).

In a recent ruling, SEC required the Chinese subsidiaries of the four largest auditing firms in the United States to submit certain documents so that the SEC could examine the quality of auditing of the Chinese listed companies in the United States by these firms. These large accounting firms are PricewaterhouseCoopers, Deloitte, Ernst & Young, and KPMG also known as the Big Four. The U.S.-based accounting firms could not produce the required documents stating that doing so would violate a Chinese law that considers such documents state secrets and prohibits making state secrets public. As a result, the SEC filed a complaint against the Big Four alleging that the firms had violated Section 106 of the Sarbanes–Oxley Act by refusing to turn over the requested documents. In a ruling on January 22, 2014, a U.S. Administrative Law Judge agreed with the SEC and ordered suspension of the affiliates of the Big Four for 6 months for practicing before SEC (Black 2014).

Clayton Act of 1914 and Mergers

The Clayton Act of 1914 created the Federal Trade Commission (FTC) and empowered the commission to regulate business conduct. Section 7 of the Act prohibits the purchase of stocks of a company by another if such purchase reduces competition in the industry. Facing the difficulties Section 7 created for companies to purchase the stocks of the target firms, many firms bypassed the law by purchasing the assets of the target. As a result, the Congress amended Section 7 in 1950 by granting the FTC the power to block asset purchases too if such purchase reduced competition.

The degree of concentration in an industry provides a guideline for antitrust law enforcement agencies in determining the level of competition. A widely used measure of concentration in an industry is the Herfindahl–Hirschman Index (HHI), which we discussed in Chapter 5. The HHI uses market shares of the companies in an industry for calculation of the degree of concentration.

The FTC will not investigate a merger if the HHI in the industry of the proposed merger is less than 1,000. An index value in the 1,000 to 1,800 interval may induce an investigation if the proposed merger would increase the HHI by 100 points. Otherwise, no investigation takes place. Finally, a proposed merger that may result in a postmerger HHI value of 1,800 or higher is considered an unacceptable concentration ratio and triggers investigation by antitrust authorities.

Postmerger Class Action Lawsuits by Shareholders in the United States

Another legal issue that cross-border acquirers of companies in the United States must consider is postmerger class action lawsuits by stockholders. As was discussed earlier, many executives of acquiring and target companies face class action lawsuits by disgruntled shareholders after completion of acquisitions. Table 15.2 shows the number of shareholder lawsuits related to acquisitions of U.S. stock companies with value of $100 million or more. The table also shows the percentage of lawsuits that were litigated. Moreover, the table shows the average number of days between the announcement of the deals and the filing of lawsuits. The number of days for filing lawsuits is indicative of the speed of class legal actions undertaken by the shareholders and their legal representatives.

The percentage of lawsuits, many of which are considered frivolous, is alarming, and should be taken into consideration in M&A strategy development and in calculating the cost of acquisition. In many of these

Table 15.2 **Number of lawsuits, and numbers and percentages of litigations related to acquisitions with value of $100 million and above in the United States**

	2009	2010	2011	2012
Number of lawsuits filed	349	792	742	602
Number of deals litigated	300 (86%)	713 (90%)	690 (93%)	560 (93%)
Average number of days between deal announcement and suit filing	14	16	17	14

Source: Daines and Koumrian (2013).

cases, the defendant pays a nuisance fee to the law firm involved, which drops the case.

The allegations for such legal actions consist of failure of the target's board of directors to fulfill its fiduciary duties by following a questionable sales process that did not result in the shareholder's wealth maximization, concluding agreements that were not based on competitive bidding, presence of the executives' conflict of interests, and failure of a target's board to disclose full information about the company to enable shareholders to make an informed choice concerning the proposed acquisition. Specifically, the complaint about inadequate information pertains to inadequacy of information about the sales process, the motivation for the board's decisions, financial predictions, and fairness of the opinion expressed by financial advisers (Daines and Koumrian 2012).

Australian Policy Toward FDI and Chinese Experiences of Direct Investment in Australia

Traditionally, Australia has welcomed foreign investment in that country under the proviso that foreign investment should be by a privately owned and operated entity without any links to foreign governments. Foreign investment in general, particularly FDI in the Australian resource sector, has played an important role in the development of the Australian economy (Drysdale and Findlay 2009). However, the rise in China's greenfield and M&A activities during the last decade in Australia, particularly Chinese direct investments in the Australian mining and energy sector, has caused public concerns about the potential adverse effects of these investments on Australian's national security and sovereignty.

To appreciate the rapid growth of China's direct investment in Australia, let us look at some figures. In 1994 to 1995, the total Chinese investment in Australia amounted to 522 million Australian dollars (Drysdale and Findlay 2009), while this sum increased to 16.190 billion Australian dollars in 2011 to 2012. Chinese investments in 2011 to 2012 involved the following sectors of the Australian economy: agriculture forestry and fishing (A$27 million), finance and insurance (A$60 million), manufacturing (A$538 million), mineral exploration and development (A$10,505 million), real estate (A$4,187 million), resource processing (A$240), services (A$634 million) (Australian Department of Treasury, 2013).

Based on the concerns of national security and sovereignty the Australian Department of Treasury, through Foreign Investment Review Board (FIRB), regulates foreign investment in Australia. However, several decisions by FIRB in blocking several direct investments by Chinese enterprises in Australia have given rise to charges of discrimination against Chinese enterprises by China's government and corporate officials (Larum 2011).

Established in 1976, mostly in response to the growing number of foreign investments in Australian natural resources, the FIRB was to advise the treasurer on merits of FDI proposals and ensure that the proposed investments safeguarded Australian national interests. The FIRB required that private foreign investment in Australian businesses be below a certain number of dollars (in late 2013, it was roughly A$250 million, and the sum is indexed to the inflation rate in Australia). Furthermore, it requires that the proposed investment does not exceed 15 percent of the assets of the Australian target company, and a maximum of 50 percent for a greenfield investment. However, investment by SOEs and Sovereign Wealth Funds (SWFs) requires review by FIRB and approval by the Australian Treasury Department regardless of the size of the proposed investment.

In cases involving SOEs and SWFs, the FIRB reviews the proposal based on the following six questions:

1. Are the investor's operations independent of foreign governments?
2. Does the investor adhere to the applicable laws and observe the standard business practices?
3. Could investment reduce competition in the industry?
4. Does the investment adversely impact Australian government's tax revenues or other policies?
5. Does the investment adversely impact Australian national security?
6. Does the investment impact the operations of an Australian business?

The Australian treasurer had publicly declared that these principles were to address Australian government and public concerns regarding independence, commerciality, and national security. The principles were to uphold economic sovereignty (Principles 1 and 2); wealth generation (Principles 3, 4, and 6) and job creation (Principle 6).

The treasurer further stated that the other aims of the principles were to promote transparency in corporate governance, a goal that cannot be achieved in the governance of SOEs. Moreover, the principles aimed to eliminate the possibility that in a market an investor acts both as the seller and the buyer of a product or natural resource, thus creating an anticompetitive environment (Huang and Austin 2011). Finally, responding to the charge of discrimination against Chinese investors, the treasurer stated that "The Guidelines are non-discriminatory—we apply them to investments by all foreign government entities. They do not target or restrict any particular country" (Larum 2011, 13).

During 2008 and 2009, a number of high-profile Chinese direct investments in Australia were scrutinized by the FIRB. In 2008, Chinalco, a Chinese SOE and leading global producer and manufacturer of metal and fabricated metal products, proposed to acquire an 18 percent interest in multinational mining company Rio Tinto (Rio) for $19 billion, with $7.2 billion convertible bonds (a loan that is convertible to share equity). Roughly about the same time of announcement of the Chinalco–Rio transaction, the Australian government introduced legislation that defined convertible notes and warranty as equity. Due to the extended regulatory oversight and conditions imposed on the proposed deal by the FIRB, Rio withdrew from the proposed acquisition deal in June 2009.[7]

Subsequent revelations of the motive behind FIRB's decisions regarding Chinese investments in Australia show that the FIRB acted to exclude Chinese investments. A news story in the *Sydney Morning Herald* stated that "The anti-China rationale was set out in confidential discussions with U.S. embassy officers in late September 2009 by the head of the Treasury Foreign Investment Division, Patrick Colmer, who is also an executive member of the Foreign Investment Review Board." The newspaper's report on the story further indicated that "The Foreign Investment Review Board told U.S. diplomats that new investment guidelines signaled 'a stricter policy aimed squarely at China's growing influence in Australia's resources sector'" (Dorling 2011).

The previous discussions support Chinese investors and government officials' view that Australia may have discriminated against Chinese direct investment in Australia. According to a survey, which asked Chinese investors and officials "why do you believe that Australia would discriminate against Chinese investment?" the respondents gave the following reasons: Australian nationalism, China is a communist country, Chinese government ownership of Australian natural resources, Chinese financing of FDI through state-owned banks, China's rapidly growing economy, and Australia is an important player in the U.S. strategy of containing China (Larum 2011).

In June 2010, the six principles were replaced by amendments to Australia's laws governing foreign investment. These principles were replaced by broader considerations, which aimed to determine whether the proposed investments are based on pure commercial interest or they are proposed with strategic geopolitical gains in mind. Furthermore, the revision considered a company government-owned if a foreign government was an owner of 15 percent or more of its assets. According to the revised rules, SOEs could acquire up to 10 percent interest in an Australian business without notifying the Australian Treasury (Larum 2011).

It should be pointed out that the increasing applications for FDI and the rising trend of approved FDI projects in Australia by the FIRB indicate that Australia is a country welcoming FDI. The trend in total applications and percentages of approved filing by the FIRB as seen in Table 15. 3 are supportive of this view.

We should point out that the applications that were not approved included withdrawals because of commercial reasons as well as burdensome requests for alteration of projects by the FIRB.

Table 15.3 Total applications considered and percentage of total applications approved by the Australian FIRB

Year	Total applications considered	Total approved	Percentage of total approved
2006–2007	7,025	6,157	88
2007–2008	8,548	7,841	92
2008–2009	5,821	5,357	92
2009–2010	4,703	4,401	93
2010–2011	10,865	10,293	95
2011–2012	11,420	10,703	94

Source: Australian Department of Treasury (2013).

Summary

This chapter began with an overview of M&A processes in China, discussing the governmental organizations that regulate China's outbound FDI. After brief discussions of the accounting method for business combinations in China, the postmerger experiences of Chinese enterprises were examined in the context of case studies of Chinese companies acquiring firms in Italy and the United States. Furthermore, governmental policies of Australia and the United States as host countries toward acquisition and inward direct investment were examined. The issue of postclosing shareholders' lawsuits as an important factor for thorough legal due diligence before any major acquisitions in the United States was also discussed.

Notes

Chapter 1

1. We note that the total exports must equal to the total imports. However, the differences in the values of imports and exports stated in the paragraph are different and the difference is due to adjustments made by the data collection organization, WTO.
2. For detailed discussions of the classification of services, see Pavitt (1984), Miozzo, and Soete (2001); and Castellacci (2008).

Chapter 2

1. For technical discussions of various types of mergers, see Chapter 5 of Reed et al. (2007)
2. Civil law is a legal system that has its intellectual roots in the Roman law and is mostly prevalent in Europe. The principles of the civil law are codified. In contrast, the common law system is based on legal precedence and the decisions made by jurists in earlier court cases.
3. See Chapter 11 for details of currency fluctuations.

Chapter 3

1. Off-balance sheet liabilities are the liabilities of the parent company that have been passed on to the subsidiaries, and do not breach the accepted accounting principles and practices.
2. For historical comparison, we also collected information on M&A share-holder litigation of deals valued over $500 million and announced in 2007 to 2009.

Chapter 5

1. Market power refers to the ability of a firm to define the prices it charges.
2. According to Ng (2013), the cost of financial due diligence ranges from $50,000 to 100,000 and takes 1 or 2 months to complete, while an audit requires 3 to 6 months and costs 5 to 10 times more than the cost of financial due diligence.
3. The discussions about the term sheet draw heavily from Ng (2013).

Chapter 6

1. For a concise discussion of differences between the two methods, see Ketz (2002).
2. A write-off of an asset is an accounting transaction, which reduces the value of an asset to 0, and its original value is considered as an expense. When an asset becomes obsolete or not usable, a write-off takes place. For example, suppose a company purchases a printer for $10,000, and after using it for 2 years a new printer is purchased. The old printer is considered obsolete, its value as an asset is entered 0 in the books, and its purchase price of $10,000 is counted as an expense.
3. A write-down is an accounting transaction that reduces the value of an asset because of damage to the asset.
4. A write-up is an accounting transaction, which increases the book value of an asset because its carrying value is less than the fair market value.

Chapter 7

1. Discussions in this chapter are heavily drawn from Weston, Mitchell, and Mulherin (2004).
2. For detailed discussions of the methods, see Chapter 10 of Brigham and Ehrhardt (2014).

Chapter 9

1. For detailed discussions of valuation of options, see Arzac (2008).

Chapter 10

1. Roughly speaking, a closed form solution to $f(x) = 0$ means that elementary expression $g(c_1, c_2, \cdots, c_p)$ such that $f\left(g(c_1, c_2, \cdots, c_p)\right) = 0$, exists.
2. An Asian option has a payoff that depends on the average price of the underlying asset for the whole or part of duration of the option.
3. We used a modified binomial method and applied it to free cash flows in valuation of real options in Chapter 9.
4. The option formulas for dividend paying stocks are different and will be discussed below. For more detailed discussions of options, see Hull (2013).
5. Note the difference between T and Δt. T refers to any length of time, for example, a week, a month, a year, and Δt refers to a very short time. Also, $t*$ refers to the expiration date of the option in the option formulas.

6. The critical observer might ask how the stock prices could have volatility if the stock exchanges are closed and no stocks are traded. To answer this question, we note that some stocks are traded after closing of the exchanges such as New York Stock Exchange. The after-hours stock trading takes place from 4 to 8 p.m. Eastern Standard Time and usually institutional stock market investors such as mutual funds are active players during the after-hours trading.

7. Technically, the formula should be $1/n$, where n is the number of years remaining until expiration of the put option. However, since we are calculating the put option at the start of the project, we have $T = \mathbf{n}$.

Chapter 11

1. A price index is a weighted average of a basket of goods and services with the quantities of purchases used as weighing factors. For a definition of weighted average, see Chapter 8.

Chapter 12

1. For detailed discussions of these components of deal structuring, see DePamphilis (2012), Chapter 11.

Chapter 13

1. According to the aim and scope of the present work, our discussions of postmerger integration present an overview of the process. For detailed discussions of all sundry aspects of postmerger integration, we refer the reader to Chapter 9 of Reed, Lajoux, and Nesvold (2007).

2. We refer the interested reader to Chapter 8 of Nickels, McHugh, and McHugh (2008) for detailed discussions of building an organization.

3. Note that we differentiate between integration strategy and integration method.

4. Just-in-time inventory control system is used in a production system in which a minimum of material inputs is kept in warehouses and materials are supplied just in time to be used on the assembly line.

5. INSEAD is the leading business school in France.

6. The term synergy refers to the notion that combining two elements leads to a sum that is greater than the sum of the individual values.

Chapter 14

1. We refer the interested reader to Sharman (2012) for discussions of and reasons for this interesting phenomenon of large Chinese capital flows to OFCs.
2. A concise definition for SOEs follows: "the term 'SOEs' refers to enterprises where the state has significant control, through full, majority, or significant minority ownership" (OECD 2005, 11).
3. International activities include both inbound and outbound M&A transactions.
4. Success in the present context differs from the use of the term in previous chapters, and implies completion of transactions.
5. Greater China includes Mainland, Hong Kong, Taiwan, and Macau.

Chapter 15

1. SASAC has SOEs at also the provincial level.
2. The following discussions concerning the SASAC rules and circular draw heavily from Norton Rose Fulbright (2014).
3. Special purpose vehicles are entities that are created to meet narrow, specific, or temporary objectives of an enterprise. These entities are used to mitigate the financial risks of the parent company.
4. For detailed discussions of the cross-border acquisition strategy of three Chinese enterprises, namely Lenovo, Huawei Technology, and Nanjing Automobile Group, see Rui and Yip (2008).
5. For detailed discussions of the Lenovo–IBM deal, see Stahl and Köster (2013).
6. According to CFIUS statistics, the filing by investors from BRICS countries as a percentage of total filings remained roughly stationary between 2010 (12 percent) and 2011 (11 percent), but rose drastically during 2012 to 27 percent.
7. The other two high-profile cases of Chinese acquisitions in Australia that were challenged by FIRB include Sinosteel–Midwest Corporation and Minmetals–OZ Minerals. See Mendelsohn and Fels (2013) for details.

References

Abramowitz, M.; and I. Stegan. 1972. *Handbook of Mathematical Functions.* New York, NY: Dover.

Accenture. 2003.

Accuval, Corporate Valuation and Advisory Services. 2013. *Intangible & Intellectual Property,* http://www.accuval.net/services/appraisals/intangible-asset-valuation.php?gclid=CJOt8L7vuboCFcxaMgodPnwAKQ#2,-1,0, (accessed October 28, 2013).

Alfred, C. Jr. Winter 1984. "The Emergence of Managerial Capitalism." *Business History Review* 58, no. 1, pp. 473–503.

Angwin, D. Spring 2001. "Mergers and Acquisitions Across European Borders: National Perspectives on Preacquisition Due Diligence and the Use of Professional Advisors." *Journal of World Business* 36, no. 1, pp. 32–57.

Arrow, K.A. 1974. *The Limits of Organization,* New York, NY: W.W. Norton & Company.

Arzac, E.R. 2008. *Valuation of Mergers. Buyouts, and Restructuring,* 2nd ed. Hoboken, NJ: Wiley & Sons.

Australian Department of Treasury. 2013. *Foreign Investment Review Board Annual Report 2011–2012,* http://www.firb.gov.au/content/Publications/AnnualReports/2011-2012/05_Chapter_2.asp, (accessed December 13, 2013).

Black, F.; and M. Scholes. May–June 1973. "The Pricing of Options and Corporate Liabilities." *The Journal of Political Economy* 81, no. 3, pp. 637–654.

Black, N. 2014. "Crouching Tiger, Hiding Auditor," *Cornell International Law Journal Online,* http://cornellilj.org/crouching-tiger-hidden-auditor/, (accessed February 21, 2014).

Bloom, N.; and J.V. Reenen. April 12, 2006. "Measuring and Explaining Management Practices Across Firms and Countries." *Centre for Economic Performance,* Discussion Paper (Identification no. 716).

Bloomberg. 2013. *Lenovo Chief Yang Shares Bonus With Workers a Second Year,* http://www.bloomberg.com/news/2013-09-01/lenovo-chief-yang-shares-bonus-with-workers-for-second-year.html, (accessed January 20, 2014).

Boateng, A.; Q. Wang; and T. Yang. June 2008. "Cross-Border M&As by Chinese Firms: An Analysis of Strategic Motives and Performance," *Thunderbird International Business Review* 50, no. 4, pp. 259–270.

Bradsher, K.; and M.J. De La Merced. December 11, 2012. "China Woos Overseas Companies, Looking for Deals." *The New York Times*, http://dealbook.nytimes.com/2012/12/11/china-woos-overseas-companies-looking-for-deals/, (April 5, 2013).

Brigham, E.F.; and M.C. Ehrhardt. 2014. *Financial Management: Theory & Practice*. 14th ed. Mason, OH: South-Western Cengage Learning.

Brock, D.M. 2005. "Multinational Acquisition Integration: The Role of National Culture in Creating Synergies." *International Business Review* 14, no. 3, pp. 269–288.

Butler, K. 2004. *Multinational Finance*. 3rd ed. Mason, OH: South-Western Cengage Learning.

Cai, X.; and H. Hu. 2012. "Outbound M&As on the Rise, Says Report." *Chinadaily.com.cn*:   http://www.chinadaily.com.cn/business/2012-12/27/content_16059362.htm, (accessed March 26, 2013).

Castellacci, F. 2008. "Technological Paradigms, Regimes, and Trajectories: Manufacturing and Service Industries in a New Taxonomy of Sectoral Patterns of Innovation." *Research Policy* 37, no. 6–7, pp. 978–994.

CFIUS (Committee on Foreign Investment in the United States). 2012. *2011 Annual Report to Congress*, http://www.treasury.gov/resource-center/international/foreign-investment/Documents/2012%20CFIUS%20Annual%20Report%20PUBLIC.pdf, (accessed January 25, 2014).

CFIUS (Committee on Foreign Investment in the United States). 2014. *2012 Annual Report to Congress*, http://www.treasury.gov/resource-center/international/foreign-investment/Documents/2013%20CFIUS%20Annual%20Report%20PUBLIC.pdf, (accessed January 24, 2014).

Chen, F.; and Y. Wang. January 2014. "Integration Risk in Cross-Border M&A Based on Internal and External Resource: Empirical Evidence From China," *Quality & Quantity* 48, no. 1, pp. 281–295.

China Daily. 2013. *Nokia Strike, Lesson for Transnational Mergers*, http://www.chinadaily.com.cn/business/2013-11/29/content_17140057.htm, (accessed November 30, 2013).

Clayton M.C.; R. Alton; C. Rising; and A. Waldeck. March 2011. "The Big Idea: The New M&A Playbook." *Harvard Business Review* 89, no. 3, pp. 48–57, http://hbr.org/2011/03/the-big-idea-the-new-ma-playbook/ar/1, (accessed October 4, 2013).

Cogman, D.; and J. Tan. 2010. *A Lighter Touch For Post-Merger Integration*, http://www.mckinsey.com/insights/corporate_finance/a_lighter_touch_for_postmerger_integration, (accessed January 22, 2014).

Covin, J.G.; and D. Slevin. May 1988. "The Influence of Organizational Structure on the Utility of an Entrepreneurial Top Management Style." *Journal of Management Studies* 25, no. 3, pp. 217–234.

Cremer, J. July 1993. "Corporate Culture and Shared Knowledge." *Industrial and Corporate Change* 2, no. 1, pp. 351–386.

Culpan, T. 2014. "Lenovo Said to Be in Advanced Discussions to Buy IBM Server Unit." *Bloomberg Businessweek*, http://www.businessweek.com/news/2014-01-20/lenovo-said-to-be-in-advanced-discussions-for-ibm-server-unit, (accessed January 20, 2014).

Daines, R.M.; and O. Koumrian. March 2012. "Recent Developments in Shareholder Litigation Involving Mergers and Acquisitions." *Cornerstone Research*, http://www.cornerstone.com/CMSPages/GetFile.aspx?guid=03dcde90-ce88-4452-a58a-b9efcc32ed71, (accessed December 30, 2013).

Daines, R.M.; and O. Koumrian. February 2013. "Shareholder Litigation Involving Mergers and Acquisitions." *Review of 2012 M&A Litigation*, http://www.cornerstone.com/files/upload/Cornerstone_Research_Shareholder_Litigation_Involving_M_and_A_Feb_2013.pdf, (accessed December 30, 2013).

Damodaran, A. 2013. *Annual Returns on Stock, T. Bonds and T. Bills: 1928–Current*, http://pages.stern.nyu.edu/~adamodar/New_Home_Page/datafile/histretSP.html, (accessed January 6, 2014).

Datta, D.K. May 1991. "Organizational Fit and Acquisition Performance: Effects of Post-Acquisition Integration." *Strategic Management Journal* 12, no. 4, pp. 281–297.

Deloitte. 2011. *China Mergers & Acquisitions Playbook: Your Reference Guide to Planning and Executing deals*, http://www.deloitte.com.mx/csgmx/docs/China_MA_Playbook.pdf, (accessed February 2, 2013).

Deloitte. 2013. *Planning to Capture Mergers and Acquisitions Operational Synergies: Perspectives on the Winning Approach*, www.deloitte.com/assets/Dcom-UnitedStates/LocalAssets/Documents/us_auto_MAOperationalSynergies POV_Part 2_11072013.pdf

Deloitte. September 30, 2013. *Post-Deal Integration: Top M&A Concern for Directors and CFOs*, http://deloitte.wsj.com/cfo/2013/09/30/post-deal-integration-directors-and-cfos-top-ma-concern/, (accessed November 4, 2013).

Deloitte. 2013. *China's Overseas Revival: 2013 Greater China Outbound M&A Spotlight*. http://www2.deloitte.com/global/en/pages/mergers-and-acquisitions/articles/china-MA-spotlight-2013.html, (accessed December 2, 2013).

DePamphilis, D.M. 2012. *Mergers, Acquisitions, and Other Restructuring Activities: An Integrated Approach to Process, Tools, Cases, and Solutions*. 6th ed. Amsterdam: Academic Press.

Department of Homeland Security. 2013. *Critical Infrastructure Sectors*, http://www.dhs.gov/critical-infrastructure-sectors, (accessed December 16, 2013).

Dik, R.; Von Lewinski, H.; Whitaker, J.; Brooks, J.; Van Wassenhove, L.; Guide, Jr., V.D.; Gritsay, V.; Lee, H.; Peleg, B.; and Whang, S. 2003. "Connecting

With the Bottom Line: A Global Study of Supply Chain Leadership and Its Contribution to the High-Performance Business." Report by Accenture.

Dorling, P. March 3, 2011. "Laws 'Aimed to Limit' Chinese Investments," *The Sydney Morning Herald*, http://www.smh.com.au/business/laws-aimed-to-limit-chinese-investments-20110302-1bexm.html, (accessed December 14, 2013).

Drysdale, P.; and C. Findlay. 2009. Chinese Foreign Direct Investment in the Australian Resource Sector. In *China's New Place in a World in Crisis*, eds. R. Garnaut; L. Song; and W.T. Woo. Canberra: ANU Press.

Durand, N. 2005. "Intellectual Property and Merger Control: Review of Recent Experience Under European Merger Regulation." *European University Institute.* http://www.eui.eu/RSCAS/Research/Competition/2005/200510-CompDurand.pdf, (accessed January 20, 2014).

Emerson, V. 2001. "An Interview With Carlos Ghosn, President of Nissan Motors, Ltd. and Industry Leader of the Year." *Journal of World Business* 36, no. 1, pp. 3–10.

Engert, O.; N. Gandhi; W. Schaninger; and J. So. 2010. *Assessing Cultural Compatibility: A McKinsey Perspective on Getting Practical About Culture in M&A.* New York, NY: McKinsey & Company.

Ernst & Young. 2011. "Toward Transaction Excellence: Ernst & Young's 2011." *Corporate Development Study*, http://www.ey.com/GL/en/Services/Transactions/Toward-transaction-excellence--Toward-transaction-excellence, (accessed November 1, 2013).

Feldman, E.J.; Feldman; and J.J. Burke. 2013. *American Suspicions Could Deter Chinese Investment*, http://www.chinaustradelawblog.com/2013/07/articles/investment/american-suspicions-could-deter-chinese-investment/, (accessed November 8, 2013).

Gomez-Meija, L.R.; and L.E. Palich. 1997. "Cultural Diversity and the Performance of Multinational Firms." *Journal of International Business Studies* 28, no. 2, pp. 309–335.

Gong, L. July 2013. "Could the Smithfield Deal Evidence a New Trend in Chinese Investment in the U.S.?" *Chadbourne & Parke LLP.* Corporate Practice Newswire.

Greenhouse, S. July 22, 2012. *At Caterpillar, Pressing Labor While Business Booms*, New York Times, http://www.nytimes.com/2012/07/23/business/profitable-caterpillar-pushes-workers-for-steep-cuts.html?pagewanted=all&_r=0, (accessed May 20, 2014).

Harrell, H.; and L. Higgins. January–February 2002. "IS Integration: Your Most Critical M&A Challenge." *The Journal of Corporate Accounting & Finance* 13, no. 2, pp. 23–31.

Haspeslagh, P.C.; and D.B. Jemison. 1991. *Managing Acquisitions: Creating Value Through Corporate Renewal.* New York, NY: The Free Press.

Hasting, P. 2013. "Shuanghui International's Acquisition of Smithfield Foods." In *China Outbound M&A Outlook*. Merger Market. http://www.mergermarket .com/pdf/China_Outbound_M&A_Outlook_2013_Eng.pdf. Date accessed November 30, 2013.

Hastings, P. 2013. *China Outbound M&A Outlook*, http://www.paulhastings.com/ publications-items/details/?id=5d2b3726-8aa5-6986-8b86-ff00008cffc3, (accessed October 10, 2013).

Hempel, C.; and M, Gilbert. May 29, 2010. "British Virgin Islands Prove Popular Among Private Equity Investors." *FIN alternatives*, http://www .finalternatives.com/node/11935, (accessed December 16, 2013).

Herd, T.; A.K. Saksena; and T.W. Steger. May 2005. "Delivering Merger Synergy: A Supply Chain Perspective on Achieving High Performance," *Accenture, Outlook Point of View*.

Hexter, J. May 2008. "Integrating Purchasing in M&A: An Interview With Lenovo's Chief Procurement Officer." *McKinsey & Company*, http://www .mckinsey.com/insights/operations/integrating_purchasing_in_m_and_a_an_ interview_with_lenovos_chief_procurement_officer, (accessed January 20, 2014).

Hopkins, H.D. 1999. "Cross-Border Mergers and Acquisitions: Global and Regional Perspectives." *Journal of International Management* 5, no. 3, pp. 207–239.

Huang, X.; and I. Austin. 2011. *Chinese Investment in Australia*. New York, NY: Palgrave-Macmillan.

Hull, J.C. 2011. *Options, Futures, and Other Derivatives*. 8th ed. Upper Saddle River, NJ: Pearson/Prentice Hall.

Hull, J.C. 2013. *Fundamentals of Futures and Options Markets*. 8th ed. Boston, MA: Prentice Hall.

Hunt, J.C. January 1990. "Changing Pattern of Acquisition Behavior in Takeover and the Consequences For Acquisition Processes." *Strategic Management Journal* 11, no. 1, pp. 69–77.

Ketz, J.E. January–February 2002. "A Critical Look at the New Purchase Accounting for M&A Transactions." *The Journal of Corporate Accounting & Finance* 13, no. 2, pp. 61–64.

Kitching, J. 1973. *Acquisitions in Europe: Causes of Corporate Successes and Failures*. Geneva: Business International.

Kitching, J. November–December 1967. "Why do Mergers Miscarry?" *Harvard Business Review* 45, no. 6, pp. 84–107.

Kuai, C. 2006. "Accounting Standards For Enterprises No. 20—Business Combinations." *Invest in China*, http://www.fdi.gov.cn/pub/FDI_EN/Laws/ law_en_info.jsp?docid=52233, (accessed April 8, 2013).

Langabeer, J.; and D. Seirfert. March 2003. "Supply Chain Integration: The Key to Merger Success (Synergy)."*Supply Chain Management Review* 7, pp. 58–64.

Larsson, R.; and S. Finkkelstein. January–February 1999. "Integrating Strategic, Organizational, and Human Resource Perspectives on Mergers and Acquisitions: A Case Survey of Synergy Realization." *Organization Science* 10, no. 1, pp. 1–26.

Larum, J. June 16, 2011. *Chinese Perspectives on Investing in Australia.* Australia: Lowy Institute.

Larum, J.; and J. Qian. 2012. "A Long March; The Australia-China Investment Relationship." *Australia China Business Council,* acbc.com.au/deploycontrol/files/upload/news_nat_fdi_report_oct.pdf, (accessed February 3, 2014).

Latham & Watkins. January 2014. *CFIUS 2012 Annual Report Reveals Increase in Chinese Filings and Notice Withdrawals,* http://www.lexology.com/library/detail.aspx?g=e40339dc-8514-41f6-ac94-dd7d462a487c&utm_source=Lexology+Daily+Newsfeed&utm_medium=HTML+email+-+Body+-+General+section&utm_campaign=Lexology+subscriber+daily+feed&utm_content=Lexology+Daily+Newsfeed+2014-01-24&utm_term=, (accessed January 24, 2014).

Lenovo. 2014. *Lenovo to Acquire Motorola Mobility From Google,* http://news.lenovo.com/article_display.cfm?article_id=1767, (accessed February 2, 2014).

Lorsch, J.; and A. Allen. 1973. *Managing Diversity and Independence.* Cambridge, MA: Division of Research, Harvard University.

Lund, S.; T. Daruvala; R. Dobbs; P. Harle; J. Kwek; and R. Falcon. 2013. "Financial Globalization: Retreat or Reset?" *Global Capital Market,* http://www.mckinsey.com/insights/global_capital_markets/financial_globalization, (accessed September 22, 2013).

Madura, J. 2013. *International Financial Management.* 11th ed. Mason, OH: South-Western/Cengage Learning.

Manatt, Phelps & Phillips, LLP. 2013. *U.S.–China M&A and Investment Outlook,* http://www.manatt.com/uploadedFiles/Content/HomePage/U.S.-China-MA-and-Investment-Outlook-2013.PDF, (accessed December 9, 2013).

Masters, J. 2013. *Foreign Investment and U.S. National Security,* http://www.cfr.org/foreign-direct-investment/foreign-investment-us-national-security/p31477, (accessed December 2, 2013).

McCann, D. 2005. "Economic Globalization and National Corporate Governance Reform." In *Governing the Corporation: Regulation and Corporate Governance in an Age of Scandal and Global Markets,* eds. J. O'Brien. Hoboken, NJ: John Wiley & Sons, LTD.

Mendelsohn, R.; and A. Fels. 2014. "Australia's Foreign Investment Review Board and the Regulation of Chinese Investment." *China Economic Journal,* 7:59–83.

Ministry of Commerce, People's Republic of China. September 2011. *2010 Statistical Bulletin of China's Outward Foreign Direct Investment,* http://english.mofcom.gov.cn/article/statistic/foreigninvestment/201109/20110907742320.shtml, (accessed December 15, 2013).

Miozzo, M.; and L. Soete. June 2001. "Internationalization of Services: A Technological Perspective." *Technological Forecasting and Social Change* 67, no. 2, pp. 159–185.

Mowery, D.C. May 1990. "The Development of Industrial Research in U.S. Manufacturing." *American Economic Review* 80, no. 2, pp. 345–349.

Nagurney, A. 2006. *Supply Chain Network Economics: Dynamics of Prices, Flows and Profits.* Cheltenham, England: Edward Elgar Publishing.

Nahavandi, A.; and A.R. Malekzadeh. January 1988. "Acculturation in Mergers and Acquisition." *Academy of Management Review* 13, no. 1, pp. 79–90.

NDRC. 2014. *Department of Foreign Capital and Overseas Investment,* http://en.ndrc.gov.cn/mfod/200812/t20081217_252124.html,http://en.ndrc.gov.cn/mfod/200812/t20081217_252124.html, (accessed January 25, 2014).

Ng, M.H.K. 2013. *Foreign Direct Investment in China: Theories and Practices.* London, UK: Routledge.

Nickels, W.G.; J.M. McHugh; and S.M. McHugh. 2008. *Understanding Business.* 8th ed. Boston, MA: McGraw-Hill/Irwin.

Norton Rose Fulbright. 2014. *New SASAC Rules to Enhance Risk Control of Chinese SOEs' Outbound Investments,* http://www.nortonrosefulbright.com/knowledge/publications/63109/new-sasac-rules-to-enhance-risk-control-of-chinese-soes-outbound-investments, (accessed January 25, 2014).

O'Brien, J. 2005. *Governing the Corporation: Regulation and Corporate Governance in an Age of Scandal and Global Markets.* Hoboken, NJ: John Wiley & Sons, LTD.

OECD. 2005. *OECD Guidelines on Corporate Governance of State-Owned Enterprises,* http://www.oecd.org/daf/ca/corporategovernanceofstate-ownedenterprises/34803211.pdf, (accessed December 7, 2013).

Olie, R. 1990. "Culture and Integration Problems in International Mergers and Acquisitions." *European Management Journal* 8, no. 2, pp. 206–215.

Pablo, A.L. August 1994. "Determinants of Acquisition Integration Level: A Decision-Making Perspective." *Academy of Management Journal* 37, no. 4, pp. 803–836.

Pavitt, K. December 1984. "Sectoral Patterns of Technical Change: Towards Taxonomy and a Theory." *Research Policy* 13, no. 6, pp. 343–373.

Ralls Corporation v. Committee on Foreign Investment in the United States, et al.; Case 1:12-cv-01513-ABJ Document 48, Civil Action No. 12-1513 (ABJ) (2013).

Ralls Corporation v. Committee on Foreign Investment in the United States, et al.; Case 1:12-cv-01513-ABJ Document 58, Civil Action No. 12-1513 (ABJ) (2013).

Ralls Corporation v. Committee on Foreign Investment in the United States, et al.; Case 1:12-cv-01513-ABJ Document 1 (2012).

Reed, S.F.; A.R. Lajoux; and H.P. Nesvold. 2007. *The Art of M&A: A Merger/Acquisition/Buyout Guide,* 4th ed. New York, NY: McGraw-Hill.

Richardson, M. 2009. *Numerical Methods for Option Pricing, Mathematical Institute.* people.maths.ox.ac.uk/richardsonm/OptionPricing.pdf, (accessed January 9, 2014).

Rui, H. and G. S. Yip. 2008. Foreign acquisitions by Chinese firms: A strategic intent perspective, Journal of World Business, 43:213–226.

SASAC. 2014. *Main Functions and Responsibilities of SASAC,* http://www.sasac .gov.cn/n2963340/n2963393/2965120.html, (accessed February 1, 2014).

Sauvant, K.; and V. Chen. 2013. *China's Regulatory Framework for Outward Direct Investment, EABER* (Working Paper No. 88), http://www.eaber.org/ sites/default/files/documents/EABER%20Working%20Paper%2088_ Sauvant%20and%20Chen.pdf, (accessed January 22, 2014).

Schlossberg, R.; and C. Laciak. 2013. Chinese Corporation Loses Court Battle Over National Security Rejection of Wind Farm Acquisition, Freshfields Bruck-haus Deringer. http://m.freshfields.com/en/insights/Chinese_Corporation_ Loses_Court_Battle_Over_National_Security_Rejection_of_Wind_Farm_ Acquisition/?LangId=2057, (accessed October 20, 2013).

Sebenius, J.K. Summer 1998. "Negotiating Cross-Border Acquisitions." *Sloan Management Review* 39, no. 4, pp. 27–41.

Securities and Exchange Commission. 2014. *The Laws That Govern the Securities Industry,* http://www.sec.gov/about/laws.shtml, (accessed February 21, 2014).

Sharman, J.C. July 2012. "Chinese Capital Flows and Offshore Financial Centers." *The Pacific Review* 25, no. 3, pp. 317–337.

Sheng, H.; and N. Zhao. 2013. *China's State-Owned Enterprises: Nature, Performance and Reform,* Hackensack, NY: World Scientific.

Shimizu, K.; M.A. Hitt; D. Vaidyanath; and V. Pisano. 2004. "Theoretical Foundations of Cross-Border Mergers and Acquisitions: A Review of Current Research and Recommendations for the Future." *Journal of International Management* 10, no. 3, pp. 307–353.

Shirivastava, P. 1986. "Post-Merger Integration." *The Journal of Business Strategy* 7, no. 1, pp. 65–76.

Song, L.; J. Yang; and Y. Zhang. July–August 2011. "State-Owned Enterprises' Outward Investment and the Structural Reform in China." *China & World Economy* 19, no. 4, pp. 38–53.

Spigarelli, F.; I. Alon; and A. Mucelli. 2013. "Chinese Overseas M&A: Overcoming Cultural and Organisational Divides." *International Journal of Technological Learning, Innovation and Development* 6, no. 1–2, pp. 190–208.

Squire Sanders Global M&A Briefing. May 2013. *China Outbound M&A,* http://www.squiresanders.com/files/Publication/d54c8c99-e6a0-425e-80d4-4d8b122b7553/Presentation/PublicationAttachment/a18546e6-281d-43d2-adbc-4e01424eed20/Squire_Sanders_Briefing_May2013.pdf, (accessed October 10, 2013).

Stahl, G.; and K. Köster. 2013. *Lenovo-IBM: Bridging Cultures, Languages, and Time Zones: An Audacious Deal (A)*, .kmi-web23.open.ac.uk:8081/download/pdf/11008070.pdf, (accessed January 20, 2014).

Sun, S.L.; Y. Zhang; and Z. Chen. May–June 2013. "The Challenges of Chinese Outward Investment in Developed Countries: The Case of CITIC Pacific's Sino Iron Project in Australia." *Thunderbird International Business Review* 55, no. 3, pp. 313–322.

Tan, K.C. March 2001. "A Framework of Supply Chain Management Literature." *European Journal of Purchasing & Supply Management* 7, no. 1, pp. 39–48.

Tayler Vinters Solicitors. 2010. *Post-Merger Integration: Do you have a Plan?*, http://www.networkedlaw.com/index.php/download_file/view/14/134/. www.networkedlaw.com/index.php/download_file/view/14/134/, (accessed January 20, 2014).

The Defense Production Act of 1950. 2009. As amended [50 U.S.C. App. § 2061 et seq], Current through P.L. 111-67, enacted September 30, 2009, http://www.fema.gov/media-library-data/20130726-1650-20490-5258/final__defense_production_act_091030.pdf, (accessed November 8, 2013).

Tyndall, G. May 2010. *Integrating Supply Chains From Business Combinations: Principles and Best Practices of Mergers and Acquisitions.* Raleigh, NC: Tompkins Associates.

United Nations. 2013. *Trends in International Migrant Stock: Migrants by Age and Sex*, http://esa.un.org/MigAge/p2k0data.asp, (accessed September 30, 2013).

United Nations Conference on Trade and Development Statistics. 2013. *Goods and Services Trade Openness, Annual, 1980-2012*, http://unctadstat.unctad .org/TableViewer/tableView.aspx, (accessed September 22, 2013). http://unctadstat.unctad.org/TableViewer/tableView.aspx?ReportId=16419

United States of America. 2007. *Foreign Investment and National Security Act of 2007.* Washington, DC: United States Government Printing Office.

Very, P.; and D.M. Schweiger. April 2001. "The Acquisition Process as a Learning Process: Evidence From a Study of Critical Problems and Solutions in Domestic and Cross Border Deals." *Journal of World Business* 36, no. 1, pp. 11–31.

Walker, D. 2005. "Restoring Trust After Recent Accountability Failures." In *Governing the Corporation*, eds. J.O. Brien. Hoboken, NJ: John Wiley & Sons.

Wang, B.; and Y. Huang. 2011. "Is there a China Model of Overseas Direct Investment?" *East Asia Forum*, http://www.eastasiaforum.org/2011/04/12/is-there-a-china-model-of-overseas-direct-investment/, (accessed December 7, 2013).

Wang, W. 2013. "Legal Analysis on the Trends and Countermeasures of Outbound Investment Performed by Chinese Enterprises." *Association of Corporate Counsel*, http://www.lexology.com/library/detail.aspx?g=77ce7b7d-af87-4c36-b910-4d4e3d092ca9&utm_source=Lexology+Daily+Newsfeed&utm_medium=HTML+email+-+Body+-+General+section&utm_

campaign=Lexology+subscriber+daily+feed&utm_content=Lexology+Daily +Newsfeed+2013-12-16&utm_term, (accessed December 24, 2013).

Wang, A.; A. Dapiran; C. Wong; H. Braun; J. Wang; and M. Thomas. 2009. "PRC Ministry of Commerce Issues New Outbound Investment Rules." *Association of Corporate Counsel,* http://www.lexology.com/library/detail. aspx?g=116ac28b-9b3c-4e1f-a53b-6c143810c9d6, (accessed April 5, 2013).

Wenbin, H.; and A. Wilkes. 2011. *Analysis of China's Overseas Investment Policies* (Working Paper No. 79), China and East Asia Node, Beijing: World Agroforestry Centre, www.cifor.org/publications/pdf_files/WPapers/WP-79CIFOR.pdf, (accessed April 5, 2013).

Weston, J.F.; M.L. Mitchell; and J.H. Mulherin. 2004. *Takeovers, Restructuring, and Corporate Governance,* 4th ed. Upper Saddle River, NJ: Pearson/Prentice Hall.

Wijnhoven, F.; T. Spila; R. Stegweea; and R.T.A. Fa. March 2006. "Post-Merger IT Integration Strategies: An IT Alignment Perspective." *Journal of Strategic Information Systems* 15, no. 1, pp. 5–28.

Wikipedia. 2014. *Cash Flow Statement,* http://en.wikipedia.org/wiki/Cash_flow_ statement, (accessed April 31, 2013).

World Trade Organization. 2013. *World Trade in Commercial Services,* http://stat .wto.org/StatisticalProgram/WSDBStatProgramHome.aspx?Language=E, (accessed December 24, 2013).

Wu, Y. April 10, 2013. "PRC MOFCOM Strengthens Strategic Planning on Outbound Investment," *Minter Ellison Alert,* http://www.minterellison .com/publications/PRC-MOFCOM-strengthens-strategic-planning-on-outbound-investment/#page=1, (accessed December 4, 2013).

Xinhua (2013) Striking Nokia workers returning to work, http://www.china. org.cn/business/2013-11/29/content_30741719.htm, 29/11/2013. Date accessed November 30, 2013.

Xiong, J; P. Schroder; and E. Tudor. 2014. *Relaxation of NDRC Rules Has Immediate Impact, but Uncertainty Remains if There Is Only Ever One Anointed Chinese Bidder,* http://www.mallesons.com//publications/marketAlerts/2014/Pages/ Relaxation-of-NDRC-rules-has-immediate-impact-but-uncertainty-remains -if-there-is-only-ever-one-anointed-Chinese-bidder.aspx#page=1, (accessed January 27, 2014).

Zarb, B.J.; and C. Noth. March 2012. "Do Integration Strategies and Supply Chain Relationships Play a Role in the Success or Failure of Mergers and Acquisitions?" *International Journal of Business and Economics Perspectives* 7, no. 1, pp. 68–81.

Zhang, J.; and H. Ebbers. 2010. "Why Half of China's Overseas Acquisitions Could Not Be Completed." *Journal of Current Chinese Affairs* 39, no. 2, pp. 101–131.

Zhu, J.; T. Boyaci; and S. Ray. 2013. *Horizontal Mergers and Supply Chain Performance,* Working Paper. Montreal, Canada: McGill University.

Index

OTHER TITLES IN OUR FINANCE AND FINANCIAL MANAGEMENT COLLECTION

John Doukas, Old Dominion University, Editor

- *Recovering from the Global Financial Crisis: Achieving Financial Stability in Times of Uncertainty* by Marianne Ojo
- *Managerial Economics: Concepts and Principles* by Donald Stengel
- *Your Macroeconomic Edge: Investing Strategies for the Post-Recession World* by Philip J. Romero
- *Working with Economic Indicators: Interpretation and Sources* by Donald Stengel and Priscilla Chaffe-Stengel
- *Innovative Pricing Strategies to Increase Profits* by Daniel Marburger
- *Regression for Economics* by Shahdad Naghshpour
- *Statistics for Economics* by Shahdad Naghshpour
- *How Strong Is Your Firm's Competitive Advantage?* by Daniel Marburger
- *A Primer on Microeconomics* by Thomas Beveridge
- *Game Theory: Anticipating Reactions for Winning Actions* by Mark L Burkey
- *A Primer on Macroeconomics* by Thomas Beveridge
- *Fundamentals of Money and Financial Systems* by Shahdad Naghshpour
- *An Executive's Guide for Moving from US GAAP to IFRS* by Peter Walton
- *Effective Financial Management: The Cornerstone for Success* by Geoff Turner
- *Financial Reporting Standards: A Decision-Making Perspective for Non-Accountants* by David Doran
- *Revenue Recognition: Principles and Practices* by Frank Beil
- *Applied International Finance: Managing Foreign Exchange Risk and International Capital Budgeting* by Thomas J. O'Brien
- *Venture Capital in Asia: Investing in Emerging Countries* by William Scheela

Announcing the Business Expert Press Digital Library

*Concise E-books Business Students Need
for Classroom and Research*

This book can also be purchased in an e-book collection by your library as
- a one-time purchase,
- that is owned forever,
- allows for simultaneous readers,
- has no restrictions on printing, and
- can be downloaded as PDFs from within the library community.

Our digital library collections are a great solution to beat the rising cost of textbooks. E-books can be loaded into their course management systems or onto students' e-book readers.

The **Business Expert Press** digital libraries are very affordable, with no obligation to buy in future years. For more information, please visit **www.businessexpertpress.com/librarians**. To set up a trial in the United States, please email **sales@businessexpertpress.com**.